Time Management for Unicorns

Time Management for Unicorns

Time and Resource Management For System Administrators

Giulio D'Agostino

BUSINESS EXPERT PRESS
Leader in applied, concise business books

Time Management for Unicorns:
Time and Resource Management For System Administrators
Copyright © Business Expert Press, LLC, 2021.

First published in 2021 by
Business Expert Press, LLC
222 East 46th Street, New York, NY 10017
www.businessexpertpress.com

ISBN-13: 978-1-95253-882-7 (paperback)
ISBN-13: 978-1-95253-883-4 (e-book)

Business Expert Press Entrepreneurship and Small Business
Management Collection

Collection ISSN: 1946-5653 (print)
Collection ISSN: 1946-5661 (electronic)

Cover image licensed by Ingram Image, StockPhotoSecrets.com
Cover and interior design by S4Carlisle Publishing Services Private Ltd.,
Chennai, India

10 9 8 7 6 5 4 3 2 1

Dedicated to my family and my wife

Description

Time is one of the most precious commodities, especially if you're the system administrator of a 'unicorn company' (a privately held startup company valued at over $1 billion). In the2018 year alone, more than 50 startups around the world attained unicorn status with a valuation of $1 billion or more, according to data from venture capital trackers like PitchBook. In this book you will find time and resource management lessons from senior system administrator Giulio D'Agostino; learn from more than 20 years experience in project management working for companies like Google, Apple, Salesforce.com and Hewlett Packard.

Keywords

time management; agile; project management; perception; behavioral psychology; salesforce; system administration; entrepreneurship; privacy; blockchain; privacy; startup; technology

Contents

Introduction

Everything we experience, every thought, impression, intention, is part of a moment in time. The world is present to us in a series of moments, like frames in a movie or the pages in this book. We seem to have no choice about this. We experience the moment we inhabit now. Time feels completely unlike space: We can't jump ahead, go back, or go forward. Time is not experienced like space, where we have a choice where to move. The difference between how we experience time and space shapes the whole of our existence.

Jorge Luis Borges and Arthur Schopenhauer once said that life and dreams are pages from the same book; to read them in order is to live, but to browse among them is to dream.

Videos, music, and books are examples of how we experience time. By reading this book, you are a creature living in time.

Consciousness exists because of the story of the self, and the dimension of time is indispensable for the awareness of the self. We know that our brains experience time through the senses and by doing so create the illusion of time over and over again, helped by memory and imagination.

CHAPTER 1

A Brief History of Time

To know how we perceive time and how we experience time, it is crucial to have a brief journey to the history of calendars. Everyone uses calendars to keep tabs on significant dates and occasions; calendars would be equal to maps for direction in space. Dates on a calendar are the coordinates of our travel through time.

1.1 A Brief History of Time and Calendars

The cycle of day and night regulated the lives of our ancestors. The story of the calendar begins with the Moon, the Sun, and the Earth, with astronomy. The cycle of the seasons was known to astronomers as the tropical year, and it could be measured accurately. The stages of the Moon measure the lunar month: New Moon, First Quarter, Full Moon, Last Month, and New Moon again. It is 29.5305888531 days long, but becoming longer by a little less than a 50th of a second per century.

You will find 12.36826639275 lunar months in a tropical year. The history of this calendar principally concerns the attempts of astronomers and mathematicians to force the tropical year and the lunar month to stick into a plot composed just of whole numbers. Most new calendars, such as those of Greece, were based upon 2 months; yet, to keep the calendar in step with the seasons, it has been necessary to insert more months now and then since 12 lunar months are 10.8751234326 days short of a tropical year. Each of those Greek city-states kept its calendar; however, along with the insertion of the months has been abandoned to the public government. Callippus, a century later, made 940 lunar months equal to 76 years, all 365 days. Hipparchus, the astronomy father, suggested a different cycle that made 304 years very similar to 3760 lunar months and 111035 days. The Metonic cycle again became prominent in the ancient Christian Church, which attached the date of Easter to the phases of the Moon. Nonetheless, it is significant that although the Greeks made immeasurable contributions, their calendar isn't one of them.

1.1.1   Ancient Egypt

The culture of Egypt left to posterity a few of the wonders of the world. The pyramids and the sphinx of Giza, the Valley of the Kings, and Tutankhamun's enigmatic tomb still confuse us. The pharaohs search for immortality, show us Egyptians unique view of time, and search for immortality. The ancient Egyptians also bequeathed the idea that's at the center of our calendar. Contrary to the Babylonians, the Greeks, and the early Romans, they based their calendar upon the Sun. As the oldest high-farming culture, Egypt was dependent upon the yearly flood of the Nile, which brought water and fertile silt to the river's floodplain. Life in Egypt was ruled by the seasons, and hence by Sunlight. The Moon played no part in the calendar. The Egyptians had 12 months, all 30 days, plus an extra 5 days at the close of the year. These 5 days were given over to celebrations and were correlated with the birthdays of the best gods of the Egyptian pantheon. The year was 365 days. They accepted the seasons would become later and later to the calendar, in a cycle that would take to finish. The Egyptians assessed the relation of their calendar to the straight year, not by observing Sirius's heliacal rising. Usually, Sirius rising was the ruler that defined Sirius's first sighting every year in the morning sky before sunrise.

Until the time of Julius Caesar, the calendar was the sole calendar in which each month and day was defined by external rules instead of being determined by priests' discretion or by the astronomers' observations.

1.1.2   Julian Calendar

The calendar of ancient Rome was mainly a lunar calendar with an extra, or intercalary, month occasionally inserted to maintain the weeks more or less in step with the seasons. You will find 12 months, and they were termed as follows: Januarius, Februarius, Martius, Aprilis, Maia, Junius, Quintilis, Sextilis, September, October, November, and December. In over 2500 decades, these titles have come down to us almost unchanged, apart from Quintilis and Sextilis. The Romans were quite superstitious. They considered odd numbers as blessed and even numbers as unlucky. So all months except February had an odd number of days: March, May, Quintilis, and October 31; February 28; and the remainder 29. This gave 355 days, approximately equivalent to 12 lunar months. When required, at the end of February, and on occasions, February itself was shortened to 23 days, the month was added. The new moon was the day of the Kalends (source of the term *calendar* itself), the moon's first quarter was the day of the Nones, and the Ides fell on the day of the full moon. The Ides was the 13th, exception made for months in which it was the 15th. You will recall that Julius Caesar was warned to beware of the Ides of March. The Romans did not count the times of the month in the way that we do. Instead, they counted toward the following of the three days called.

In a 31-day month such as March, the "Nones" fell on day 7. The day before the "Nones" was Pridie Nonas Martias, which translates into "the day before the Nones of March." The Nones itself was contained in this countdown, which is why the fifth is known as the day before the Nones rather than the second. After the Ides, the dates had been counted down to the Kalends of the following month, so that March 16 was appointed ante diem XVII Kalendas Aprilis or even "the 17th day before the Kalends of April," although it was known as part of the month of March. The Romans believed that certain days were more reassuring than many others for carrying out significant events such as business contracts, religious rites, and battles. The priests, led by the Pontifex Maximus (the chief high priest of the College of Pontiffs in ancient Rome), would inform a Roman citizen if a specified day was not included in the calendar, and naturally, they left a fee for each query to add a day to the official Catholic calendar. The priests decided when months were required; therefore, they had total control over every aspect of personal and public life throughout the calendar. They had no formal rules to tell them when intercalation was needed. In any case, they were somewhat dismissive, so that by the time Julius Caesar became Pontifex Maximus, the calendar had slipped by nearly 3 months in relation to the seasons. To be able to bring the calendar back into line with the seasons, Caesar ordered that 3 intercalary months must be added at the end of the year, which we know as 46 BC. However,

Caesar's most important reform was to reject the lunar month entirely and embrace a solar year whose average length was 365.25 days. He introduced the cycle of leap years, and that we use today. The extra day was added at the end of the Roman year. Once again, carelessness prevailed. The intercalation was not employed by the priests every 3 years, maybe 4. It originated from the superstition that four is an even number, and hence unlucky. Augustus Caesar fixed the mistake by omitting leap years before AD 8, and also, the Julian calendar was retained without further change before the substantial reform of Pope Gregory XIII in 1582.

1.1.3   The Week

From the Bible, the creation of the Earth takes 6 days, and God rests on the seventh. It is difficult to follow the ultimate source of the 7-day week, but in the calendar, the 7th, 14th, 19th, 21st, and 28th days of every month were set aside for rest. After the Exile, the Jewish calendar adopted the titles of the Babylonian months, and likely, the week was also introduced into Judaism at this time. There was an 8-day cycle involving market days. It was only in the second century BC that a 7-day cycle became predominant, which may have owed to more than Hebrew or Babylonian influences. Astrologers recognized seven planets (like the Sun and the Moon) and assigned a single planet to rule each of the 24 hours of this day, at a constant sequence. The planet that ruled the very first hour of the day was taken to rule over the whole day, and this gave rise to a 7- day cycle. The Romans started to name each day following its ruling planet: Saturn's day, the Sun's afternoon, the Moon's day, Mars's day, Mercury's day, Jupiter's day, Venus's day. From the Romance languages, the link is evident. In the Germanic languages, the names of the Norse Gods Tiu, Woden, Thor, and Freya were replaced by Mars, Mercury, Jupiter, and Venus.

Jewish tradition initially had no names for the days of the week. It is not possible to say whether the cycle of times of the week has lasted without interruption since Roman times. The Gregorian calendar reform, even though it removed 10 days from the calendar at a stroke, preserved the sequence of times of this week.

Anno Urbis Conditae is used to refer to a given year in Ancient Rome. A Roman date would give the names of the two people who functioned in that year as consuls. The year of the reign of their king or queen dates British Acts of Parliament. In the United States, presidential decrees are dated by the year because of the foundation of the republic in 1776. It appears natural to measure the passage of years from some event. In about the year AD 530, a monk named Dionysius Exiguus — "Denis the Small" from Scythia in southwest Russia, introduced the Anno DominiOffsite Link (AD) era, which is used by certain people to number the years of both the Gregorian calendar and the (Christianized) Julian calendar. As many scholars of the time, Dionysius was worried about the exact calculation of the date of Easter, and he built a table of Easter dates for 19 years. At that time, years had been quantified from the start of the reign of the Emperor Diocletian, centuries earlier. Dionysius determined that Anno Diocletian 248 was 532 years since the birth of Jesus Christ. And because Easter commemorates the most significant event in the Christian faith, Dionysius invented the Anno Domini dating, which was used to number the years of both the Gregorian calendar and the Julian calendar. Dionysius discovered its first winner in the 18th-century historian, the Venerable Bede, who used it in his *Ecclesiastical History of the English People*. Several versions of Anno Domini were used: *Anno Incarnationis Dominicae*, from the year of "Our Lord's incarnation"; *Anno a Nativitate*, in the year following the "Nativity"; *Anno a Passione*, in the year following the "Passion"; Anno Gratiae, from the year of "Grace"; *Anno salutae Humanae*, from the year of "human redemption." Historians and theologians agree that Dionysius made an error in calculating the year of Christ's birth. The historical evidence makes it hard to know whether the Nativity happened later than roughly 4 BC, because that was the year in which Herod the Great is known to have died.

There's also astronomical evidence on a date in 7 BC that connects the Star of Bethlehem with a conjunction of Jupiter and Saturn, an event that would happen to be of the maximum significance to astrologers because it meant that the two planets approached one another at the sky three times in just 6 months.

1.1.4 The Christian Calendar

In the calendars, years are counted from the birth of Christ, celebrated on December 25. The other significant events in the Christian religion are the Crucifixion and the Resurrection of Christ. This is the event that gives each Christian meaning and hope. The Crucifixion and the Resurrection are celebrated at Easter. From the early Church, these were the events that led Christianity irrevocably away from Judaism. Also, for almost 700 years, the date of Easter was the subject of debate and potential schism. The Jewish calendar was a lunar calendar, the month's beginning was marked with the new crescent Moon; therefore, the 14th day belonged to the Full Moon.

Additionally, Nisan was the first month of the year, which was organized such that the new year started at the Spring Equinox. The Christians, recalling their Jewish origins, continued to celebrate Easter at the time of Passover. They, just as the Jewish community itself, couldn't say in advance when Passover would occur. There were two opposite views: The Jewish heritage still strongly influenced one group, that is, the Passover must fall on the 14th day of the lunar month. Their insistence on the importance of the number 14 led to them being named Quartodecimians. The other group believed that the party of Easter must follow the events of the Holy Week, with the Crucifixion on Friday and the Resurrection on the following Sunday. The Western Church observed Easter on Sunday, no matter the numerical date of the month. The Eastern Church observed Easter on the 14th day of the month. This quarrel threatened to lead to a schism, and it was one reason that in AD 325 led Constantine the Great to summon the leaders of both the Eastern and Western Churches to the Council of Nicaea. This council is best remembered for the Nicene Creed, the significant announcement of Christian belief, but also, it agreed on the formula for determining the date of Easter.

The council decreed that Easter must be the first Sunday after the complete Moon after the Spring Equinox, March 21; however, if that Full Moon fell on a Sunday, then Easter should be the Sunday after. The final phrases hint at the depth of this disagreement, for it was possible that Easter could be celebrated at the time of the Full Moon, the 14th day of the lunar month, which had been the Quartodecimian opinion. Even after the Council of Nicaea, the issue was not settled. The astronomers knew of at least four cycles that connected the year, and the lunar. There was a bi-cycle, which equated 8 decades to 99 lunar months. There was the Metonic cycle, which made equal to 235 lunar months, 19 years. One thousand thirty-nine lunar weeks were matched to 84 years by the Roman cycle. Finally, the cycle devised by Victorius in AD 457 took the 19-year Metonic cycle and the 28-year cycle of times of the week within the Julian calendar and created a cycle of 532 decades. Rome utilized the Victorian cycle, but the Church in Ireland and Britain, which had always looked to its Celtic roots, preferred the Roman cycle of 84 years.

The calendar of Julius Caesar has been an attempt to make the length of the calendar year match the period of the seasons. Its simplicity—including an excess day to February—has been its virtue. The monk Dionysius Exiguus calculated the year of the Nativity in a manner that leap years Anno Domini are those that are divisible by just four, and this is an easy rule to remember. But this simplicity comes at a price: Four years of the Julian calendar are equivalent to 1,461 times, so the average length of the year is 365.25 days. This is 11 minutes more than the suitable period for the tropical season. It may not seem significantly less long than the time it takes to boil water in a kettle and make a cup of tea, but each season is 15 minutes, and the discrepancy builds up. After just 128 years, it turns into a whole day. The seasons start on the calendar. The ancient Egyptians lived very happily with a calendar that allowed the seasons every 4 years to slip by a day. The Romans and the Greeks were satisfied to live with the random intercalation required by a lunar calendar. Even the Christian Church had fought bitter internal battles over the calendar, especially over the date of Easter.

As early as the 8th century, we no longer fell on the day allotted to Easter by the Council of Nicaea. By the early Middle Ages, astronomers agreed something must be done, but to alter the calendar was not a measure that could be dismissed. Successive popes researched the problem and declined to act. It fell to Pope Gregory XIII to fix the error, to ensure that future generations wouldn't face the same dilemma. Pope Gregory XIII was born Ugo Boncompagni in 1502. He studied law and became a judge and a lecturer in his native town. In 1549 he had been sent into the Council of Trent, an ecumenical council that met fitfully to talk about matters of significance to the Roman Church. In 1565, Ugo became pope and was elected a cardinal. Gregory sent a letter labeled *Compendium novae rationis restituendi Kalendarium*, describing his suggestion for reforming the calendar. From 1582, aged 80, he was prepared to act. He also issued the apostolic letter "Inter Gravissimus," which ensured his place alongside Julius Caesar as a man who might enforce his will on the very course of time itself. The title of the apostolic letter means "one of the most serious" and is removed in the first sentence of the letter. In total, this reads as follows: "Among the most, jobs that are acute continue perhaps but at the least of these which we have to attend to, would be to finish with the assistance of God what Trent's Council has reserved to the Apostolic See." In December 1563, the final session of the Council of Trent had completed the reform of the Mass along with the breviary. The latter included a provisional calendar reform, intended to fix the calendar's forecasts of the dates of the New Moon, which by then were four times out of step with the real Moon. New discrepancies were prevented by the addition of a leap day from 1800 onward. Among its most assiduous members was Christopher Clavius. TThe council had recommended that the pope be embraced in the Inter Gravissimus. To restore the date set by the Council of Nicaea, for March 21, was omitted from the calendar in October 1582. Times of this week's cycle were not disrupted, but October did not exist in the year 1582.

In order to draw the average length of the calendar year into closer agreement with the length of the year, 3 leap years were to be omitted in every 4 centuries. Every centurial year that was not divisible by 400 would not overlap the year. This was a smart ploy. The next year that was centurial was 1600, only 18 decades away at the time of the Inter Gravissimus; also, it might be a leap year in the calendar and the older. Nobody living through Gregory's calendar reform would need to be concerned about the guideline for leap years. Yet, it had the impact of making 400 years equivalent to 14,6097 days, providing an average calendar year of 365.25 days, just 26.8 seconds longer than the tropical year. This difference would amount to 1 day in 3,200 years.

As the leap year rule meant the days of the week could repeat every 28 years, the cycle of Victorius could no longer be employed to construct tables of the dates of Easter. A new way of calculating Easter needed to be devised, and it took a set of corrections that are arcane to permit for the fact that the proportion of the length of this calendar year to that of the lunar month had changed. The dates of Easter in the calendar would also be changed to repeat every year cyclically.

The calendar was accepted without delay in Italy, Poland, Spain, and Portugal, all of which embraced it in the Inter Gravissimus, on the date stipulated. France and Belgium moved into the calendar in December 1582. The areas of Germany, Austria, and Switzerland moved through 1583 and 1584; some regions of those countries waited until 1701. From the Church of Rome, memories were still fresh in 1582 of Henry VIII's split in England. A pope had excommunicated Elizabeth in just such an apostolic letter as the Inter Gravissimus. The calendar reform met a similar attitude on the part of the secular authorities. The queen referred the issue to John Dee, a noted mathematician, who responded favorably.

Dee's verdict was passed in turn. Dee was endorsed by the Queen and the Pope. The matter was subsequently referred in March 1583 to the Archbishop of Canterbury, who had been encouraged to confer with his bishops and come back with a reply as soon as possible, since the queen meant to proclaim in May of the following year the adoption of this new calendar. The queen and her ministers did not obtain the reply that they had hoped for. The English churchmen's response was deceptive from the pope, who had been denounced as the Antichrist. It had been argued that what was performed by the Council of Nicaea could only be undone by another council. The Council of Trent was not such a council, and they could never enter into dialogue since the churches believed that the pope was Antichrist. There might be no second Council of Nicaea. England would keep the Old Calendar for another 170 decades, ten days (11 from 1,700) supporting the rest of Europe and celebrating the New Year on March 25. Letters to Europe took one in the Old Style two dates and one in the New Style.

The regular procession of leap years is changed only three times at 4100 years. Nearly two centuries may elapse (e.g., from 1901 to 2099) through which the Julian leap year principle applies. And the Gregorian calendar will keep a step before a day's correction is needed again. In the wake of the calendrical reform, considerations were secondary to the zeal to throw everything that stayed the citizens of the yoke of the monarchy and the church. Hence, the Gregorian calendar was replaced by person with no allegiance to religion.

Astronomers and mathematicians created the Gregorian calendar, and were lauded as part of the new Age of Reason. It had 12 equivalent weeks of 7 days, plus 5 or 6 festive days at the year's close. Each month was divided into years or three 10-day weeks.

1.2   How Do We Experience Time?

As time is something different from experienced events, we do not perceive time as such, but as one-dimensional series of frames. However, arguably, we do not just perceive events, but also their temporal connections. So, just as it is normal to say that we perceive spatial distances and other relations between objects, could we perceive a relation between two occasions without even understanding the events?

There is then a paradox in the idea of perceiving an event as happening after another, as several events happen simultaneously while experiencing only our line of time. One of the earliest, and most famous, talks of this nature and expertise of time happens in the autobiographical *Confessions* of St Augustine. In his early years, he had rejected Christianity but was eventually converted at the age of 32. Book XI of the *Confessions* includes a lengthy and intriguing exploration of time and its relation to God. Throughout this, Augustine raises the following question: "When we say that an event or period is short or long, what is it that is being clarified as short or long?" It cannot be what is Past, as it has ceased to be, and what is nonexistent cannot presently have some properties, such as being long. Nevertheless, neither is it what is current, for now, has no duration. Whatever the case, while an event is still going on, its length cannot be assessed. Augustine's answer to the riddle is that what we measure when we measure the duration of an event or a period, is in memory. While not following Augustine into the mind dependence of different times, we can concede that the perception of temporal length is crucially bound up with memory. It is a characteristic of the memory of this event (and perhaps particularly our memory of the start and end of the event) that allows us to produce a belief about its duration. This process does not need to be described, as Augustine describes it, as a matter of measuring something entirely from the mind. Arguably, at least, we measure the occasion or period itself, a mind-independent thing, but doing so employing some psychological procedure. That there is a close relationship here is entailed by the plausible suggestion that we stipulate (albeit subconsciously) the length of the event, once it has stopped, from information about how long ago the beginning of this event happened. The question is how we acquire this information's advice. It might be indirect or direct, a contrast we can illustrate by two models of time memory described by Friedman. He calls the first time the "strength version of time." The longer ago the event, the weaker the memory trace. It provides a straightforward and direct way of assessing the length of an event. Some memories of current events may fade more quickly than memories of distant occasions, mostly when those personal events were rather conspicuous ones (visiting a seldom seen and frightening comparative when one was a young child, as an example). A contrasting account of time is your "inference version." Following the time, an event is not only read from some aspect of the memory of it but is inferred from data about relations between the occasion in question and other occasions whose date or time is understood. The "Inference model" may be plausible when we are observing remote events, but less so for much more recent ones. Additionally, the model posits a somewhat complex cognitive operation that is not likely to occur in nonhuman creatures, such as the rat. In this, a given response will postpone the incidence of an electrical shock by a fixed time, for example, 40 seconds, called the R–S (response–shock) interval. Eventually, the speed of reacting tracks the R–S interval, so that the likelihood of reacting increases rapidly as the conclusion of the interval approaches. It is hard to avoid the inference here that only the passing of time is acting as a conditioned stimulus—that the rats, to put it in more anthropocentric conditions, are estimating periods. In cases like this, the strength model seems more appropriate compared with the inference model. The term "specious present" was introduced by the psychologist E.R. Clay. However, the best-known characterization of this was by William James, widely considered as one of the founders of modern psychology. How long is this specious gift? Elsewhere in the same function, James asserts, "We are constantly aware of a certain duration—the specious present—varying from a couple of seconds to probably not more than a minute. This duration (using its content perceived as having one component earlier and yet another part afterward) is the initial instinct of time." This sudden variation in the period of the specious present makes one suspect more than one definition is hidden in James's rather vague characterization. There are two sources of ambiguity here: One is over whether "the specious present" refers to the aim of the experience, namely, a period in time, or how that object is introduced to us. "The next is over how we should interpret immediately sensible." Several studies suggest that the specious present is the duration itself, picked out as the thing of a specific sort of experience. However, "instantly sensible" admits of several disambiguations. We might perceive as present items that exist. Really, given the finite speed of the transmission of both light and sound (and the finite speed of transmission of data from receptors to mind), it appears that we only ever perceive what is past. Nevertheless, this will not by itself tell us what it is to perceive something as current, rather than as past. Nor does it clarify the most striking feature of our experience, as of the gift: that it is constantly changing. The passing (or apparent passage) of time is its most striking characteristic, and in any situation, our experience of time must account for this aspect of our experience. The first problem is to explain our temporal experience is restricted in a way in which our spatial experience is not. Our experience is not restricted to the immediate vicinity (although, of course, our experience is spatially limited to the scope that sufficiently distant objects are invisible to us). We can perceive objects that exist in a variety of spatial connections to us: near, far, to the left or right, down or up. However, even though we perceive the past, we do not perceive it, but as the current. Moreover, our expertise does not only seem to be temporally limited, but it is also such that we do not comprehend the future, and we do not continue to comprehend transient events long after information from them reached our senses. Now, there is a straightforward reply to this question of why we do not perceive the near future, and it is a casual one. Perception is a causal process, so to perceive something is to be causally affected by it; hence, we can only perceive earlier events, never subsequent ones. We could refer to the principle that there could be no action at a temporal distance, so that something distant past can only randomly influence us via more proximate occasions. One temporal boundary of our experience is solved. What about the other? There seems no credible reason why people should not directly go through the distant past. To perceive something as a present is to comprehend it. We do not need to postulate some excess items in our experience that are "the experience of presentness." It follows that there could be no "understanding of pastness." Also, in case pastness was something we could perceive, then we would perceive everything in this manner since every occasion is "Past: by the time we perceive it." Nevertheless, even if we never perceive anything as past (at the same time as perceiving the case in question), we could intelligibly talk more widely of the experience of pastness: the experience we get as it pertains to a conclusion. Moreover, it has been implied that a feeling of pastness accompanies memories, more especially, episodic memories, those of our experiences of previous events. The difficulty that this proposal is supposed to resolve is that episodic memory is merely a memory of an event; it signifies the event simpliciter, rather than the fact that the event is past. An alternative account, and one that does not appeal to some phenomenological aspects of memory, is that memories get us to form past-tense beliefs, and it is by this that they represent an occasion as past. How can we perceive precedence among occasions? A temptingly simple response is that the perception of precedence is merely a sensation brought on by instances of precedence, as instances of redness cause a sensation of red. We can differentiate the two cases; therefore, it cannot merely be a matter of perceiving a relation, but something related to our understanding of the relation. Nevertheless, the mere perception of the relation cannot be all there is to perceiving precedence. We first perceive the hour hand at one position, say pointing to 6 o'clock, and we perceive it at another place, pointing to half-past 6. So I have got two perceptions, one later than another. I might also be aware of the temporal relationship of both positions of the hand. However, I do not perceive that connection, in that I do not see the hand moving. By comparison, I do see the second hand move from one place to another: "I see the successive positions as successive." In giving an account of the numerous facets of time understanding, we inevitably take advantage of theories that we take to get a goal counterpart in the world: the past, real-time order, causation, mutation, the passage of time, and so forth. However, one of the essential lessons of doctrine, for many authors, is that there could be a gap between our representation of the world and the planet itself. (It would be reasonable to add that, for other writers, this is precisely not the lesson philosophy teaches.) Indeed, it is intriguing to note how many philosophers have taken the view that, despite appearances, time, or any facet of time, it is unreal. In this final segment, we will take a look at how three metaphysical disagreements regarding the nature of the world socialize with balances of time understanding.

1.3   Time Perception in Philosophy and Science

The understanding of time is essential to our expertise and fundamental to virtually all our actions. Correspondingly, time perception was among the earliest themes of experimental psychology and was extensively studied for well over a century. Philosophers have usually approached the idea of the timing of experiences by addressing the question of how the experiences of temporal phenomena could be explained. As a result, the dilemma of timing was addressed in two distinct ways. Like the questions introduced in sciences, the first concerns the connection between the seasoned time of events and the real-time of occasions. The second strategy is much more specific to philosophers' debates and concerns that the phenomenology of encounters: is the apparent temporal arrangement of encounters. Philosophers are more concerned with the phenomenology and the metaphysics of time compared with scientists, who often focus on performance, particularly time-order tasks, and measure the timing of encounters in milliseconds. Philosophical notions of time consciousness, which aim to account for how time and temporal possessions figure in our consciousness as well as contents of extraordinary states, may be classified into roughly three categories.

The first, the *snapshot view*, is like a straightforward viewpoint. Many scientific theories regarding the timing of experiences concur with this thesis, even when they reject another realistic view thesis. A few philosophers reject the snapshot view because accounting for rectal experiences has shown difficulty within this framework.

Temporal experiences are the ones that indicate the passage of time. More recently, philosophers have focused on experiences of movement, succession, and persistence. Thus consider, for example, an adventure of motion. If we only experience what is taking place on a snapshot, then our experience using a moving object consists of the thing in only one of its just-past (or predicted) positions—the experience of movement is missing. Additionally, while the picture view allows for a succession of adventures, this does not yet amount to the adventure of the series. If a series is something that we can encounter, then it seems that the snapshot view cannot account for this. Likewise, we could never really encounter melody if our experience consisted of the notes being played. Instead, movement, for instance, is only inferred based on our memories of their previous positions of stimulation and our perception of their current location. Regardless of this, the picture view does not involve the rejection of temporal encounters.

Contemporary philosophers, however, take for granted the phenomenology related to temporally extended events. Hence, they assert that we can experience change, movement, and other dynamic events with the same immediacy we experience colors and shapes. Because of this, the cinematic version is rejected. Given that the version is not usually separated from the photo view, the latter can be reversed. The idea that an experience covers a temporal interval enables experiential contents that seem (to get a subject) to happen at various times to be parts of a single experience. In this frame, the experience of a single flash succeeding another could be described as follows: When we encounter the last flash, the first flash lingers in our understanding of past or previous content. Since we are conscious of the two flashes during the same specious present, we also experience the succession. It does not mean that the experience itself would be temporally structured in a feeling it has temporal parts just that, to a topic, the funniest contents within one specious present seem as if embedded in a dynamic arrangement. Saying that the contents of expertise are temporally extended is much more a description of temporal adventures than an explanation of them.

The supplied explanations come in two major models, which form the remaining two groups of the philosophical notions of time consciousness. The first is your intentionalist version (or intentionalist model), based on which encounters take place, objectively speaking, in snapshots. In more concrete terms, our experience of succession is considered to come about by having two experiential contents appear to be in series on a single near-momentary experience. It is achieved when the first experiential content is presented as something that only occurred (retained content), while the other is introduced as current content (primal image). The competing perspective, the extensionist version, maintains that both the experiences and their contents are temporally extended. Thus, our experience of succession comes about when two experiential contents that occur in succession are perceived as the contents of one experience. Thus, what separates the two models is their stance on the relationship between the possessions of an adventure and its contents.

As mentioned previously, for reasons linked to temporal phenomenology, philosophers have been rather univocal in their rejection of the thesis of instantaneous contents. Therefore, philosophers reject at least two of the three theses that include a straightforward view. I think the easy view could be defended, nevertheless. Such protection comes in the form of two other perspectives, which, in my opinion, are sound and at least as empirically well grounded because of their alternatives. The first one, the quick snapshot view, describes the phenomenology in the framework of a photo view—at the frame that the thesis of instant contents renders us. The dynamic snapshot view, as its title suggests, subscribes to the thesis of instantaneous contents. The majority of philosophers have rebuffed this thesis as it has been maintained; it contributes to Phenomeno-temporal Antirealism. Hence, a philosophical model endorsing the thesis needs to provide a convincing argument of why there is not any temporal phenomenology or demonstrate how the thesis could be harmonious with the precision of temporal phenomenology. While the cinematic model takes the first route and has had little success in doing this, the quick snapshot view attempts to provide the demonstration of compatibility known. This usually means that a snapshot can (but does not need to) contain contents that a frame in a movie does not let (namely, cerebral phenomenology). The main difficulty here is, of course, the rectal phenomenology cannot be explained in the same manner as in the extensionist and re-intentionalist models. Because the quick snapshot view maintains that the contents of our experiences are not temporally extended, it cannot appeal to the thought that a single experience includes contents that subjectively seem to occur at several times. Instead, the quick photograph view holds that such contents are not required for rectal phenomenology to happen. The dynamic snapshot view holds that rectal phenomenology can be explained similarly, namely, by appealing to the existence of mechanics specific to various types of temporal phenomenology. Thus, our experiences of causality, change, movement, succession, and so forth would be due to mechanisms separate from each other and subsequently also separate from general mechanisms such as working memory. It is where the quick snapshot view differs from Le Poidevin's place, as he accounts for rectal experiences aside from motion by appealing to the memory.

The human brain is not like the measuring devices in classical physics: There is not any immutable mapping between outside magnitudes and inner sensations that can be obtained by pure mathematical approaches. The basis and generality of the linear property of time remain topics of considerable debate, together with scale invariance variously attributed to this pulse rate of a dedicated pacemaker, the transfer of rectal representations into memory, or even the emergent properties of low-level interactions between neurons in the human brain.

However, recent work is identifying instances where distinct subgroups of participants, ostensibly from precisely the same population, nonetheless show substantial heterogeneity even for well-established consequences. One instance comes from the widely reported discovering that novel stimuli (*oddballs*) have longer subjective length compared with replicated items. This finding has been found in several experiments using various techniques and is robust enough to be regarded as a standard *temporal illusion*.

CHAPTER 2

Business Time

2.1   Business Time

Although everyone gets pretty much the same amount of hours to work with daily, what people do not have in equivalent amounts are other valuable assets: ability, intelligence, money, ambition, energy, passion, attitude, even outlook. All these exceptional reserves play into your very best use of time. So the better you understand yourself—your strengths, weaknesses, goals, values, and motives—the easier it is to manage your time efficiently. In this part, you look at your strengths and goals, consider how much your time is worth, and observe personal motivation and behavior patterns that influence your focus during the day. The chances are that you have discovered some skills that you come to or perhaps have worked hard to get by this point in your life. Maybe you're a master negotiator. You might be a good writer. Whatever your strengths, developing the handful that provides you with the most return on your efforts, pushing you forward to attain your goals, is a more productive course of action than trying to be the best at everything. For many people, these strengths typically number no higher than half a dozen. In addition to underlining your strengths, you need to identify the areas where your skills are lackluster, and then, determine which tasks are essential for meeting the goals you wish to accomplish and build the relevant skills. Invest time in honing and keeping your strengths, and address the weaknesses that you want to overcome to reach your targets.

Using your dreams to fire up your time management success means you have to identify your goals and keep them in focus. Pinning down what is most important to you will require some soul searching. Write your goals down—all of them.

Most people consider the value of their time as it pertains to on-the-job activity. The fast-food employee knows he earns a minimum wage per hour. The freelance artist advertises a per-hour rate. But to be genuinely conscious of the value of your time, you want to carry this notion into your private life as well. The amount of time in your personal life is as valuable as that in your work life. Consistently, private time is priceless.

If you know your rhythms—when you're most focused, what times of the day you are best equipped to tackle specific tasks—you can perform your most important activities when you're in the zone. Everyone works at a different pace, and recognizing that rhythm is among the most valuable personal discoveries you can make.

Effective time management requires more than high intent and self-knowledge. To keep your time under control, you need a framework. Establishing a reliable system you can replicate is a key to succeeding in managing your time. Methods, standards, strategies, and guidelines protect your time and permit you to use it to your best advantage.

A good system of time management demands order and organization. Creating order in your mind saves time wasted searching for things, from significant phone numbers to your shoes. But even more, physical order generates mental requests and makes it possible to perform more efficiently. Yes, your workspace should be clean and organized, with documents and folders organized in some sequence, which makes items easy and quick to discover. Your desk should be clean and minimal, providing space to work.

Communicating effectively is one of the best ways to manage your time. Among the biggest wastes of company time is, no surprise, speaking with co-workers. But what may be a surprise is that the abuse is not a function of weekend catch-up discussions that occur at the coffee machine or the gossip gathering at the copy machine. Instead, it's the banter at the weekly staff status reports, the drawn-out updates of jobs that never seem to conclude, the sales presentations that go off track. It's all of the meetings that could be as short as 10 minutes but take an hour or longer.

Interruptions creep into a workday in all kinds of insidious manners. You now have more of those interruptions than ever before. You get sidetracked by instant messaging and social media such as Instagram and Twitter. The listing of 5-minute here-and-there breaks is endless. Study after study affirms that multitasking isn't the best work style. The constant stops and starts disrupt a project, requiring startup time every time you turn back to the job. I truly believe being a good time manager at work depends on how you create, craft, and implement your disturbance system and strategy. Every day, interruptions cost hours of lost productivity for businesses. Also, remember, procrastination has a lot of causes, but the majority of the reasons to procrastinate leave you headed for trouble.

Several factors create confusion and uncertainty that keep you from making effective but quick decisions. Often, part of the struggle has many alternatives to choose from.

Maintaining control of your time in the office requires you to develop some methods to manage meetings, appointments, and other work interactions, so they are as efficient and productive as possible. Whether you commence the communication or you are merely a participant, you can have some control over the meeting.

Throughout the process of working to improve how you manage your time, you'll occasionally encounter points where you begin feeling disappointed, wondering if your efforts are paying off. Whenever you hit these lows—and you will—remember to give yourself credit for every step you take in the ideal direction. Take motivation to the next level by involving others in the reward. Let your family know that a day out expects in the event you meet your week's goals before the deadline.

Work always expands to fill the time you allow for it. Regardless of how successful I am, whether I have just a couple things to accomplish or a sky-high pile on my desk and whether I leave work on time or stay late, there is always something that does not get done.

Turn chaos into productivity, literally: the power of routines!

Routines and habits are some of the most powerful ways of managing time. When we want to multitask, we are lowering the quality of how we experience time: When we do two things at the same time, we are doing two separate things.

Our brains are designed to separate tasks.

Since we experience time in a one-directional/dimensional way, we need to make sure to open-plan *time blocks*.

Once we become aware of the obstacles to master our time, we need to define a point where to start *doing things*. Start with the big ideas/the high-level stuff and see where that takes you. Make sure you are prioritizing the right high-level stuff.

A bad example of a prioritization strategy is what happens daily in our personal lives. Most people have a list of things that they need to choose from, and it might look like this:

- Finances
- Health
- Personal life
- Job
- Family
- Relationships

The reality is we don't need to focus on all of them; the problem is that it will take time to see which one of them we should focus on that the others will become easier (or just consequences).

Again, the high-level approach wins.

Let's take a step back for a moment and consider *psychological time*. Psychological time is often mixed with the experience of self-awareness. Forms of psychological time are Memory (history of the self, health), Awareness (the self, outside world), Persistence (patterns, habits), Feedback (growth, introspection), and Trends (the where, the who and the micro versus macro).

When experiencing time indirectly, without wasting it in the process of observation, we notice that successful paths and rewarding careers are not the ones constrained by micromanagement or over planning.

As four-dimensional beings, we perform and grow better when we are ready for opportunities, and if we are prepared and wise with our time, we can turn them into achievements.

When we are *caught in time*, we often forget the relevance of defining a *block of minutes* (or hours) to observe where to start and which decisions with high-level consequences require our immediate attention.

We do know that we often try to fill in every single slot of our time with *important stuff to do*, even though we know that better communication between teams or collaborators and a clear vision of the final goal would have created spaces between those rushed tasks in our busy lives.

Almost always the prework steps (training, forecasting, etc.) are the ones that a lot of companies and entrepreneurs want to skip because they are outside their comfort zones (the sales department that wants to jump into action or the young entrepreneur who looks for quick investments with no real cash flow).

Great answers live outside comfort zones. Connect priorities, passion, and dedication, and your overall perception of time will change; you will start to own time rather than be owned by time.

2.2   Action Items

- One Task at a Time: Spend time on a critical task at a time. This will require putting the cell phone away and on not disturbing and silent modes.
- The 80/20 Rule: Only 20 percent of the tasks you spend time performing produce 80 percent of the results you want to achieve. Therefore, prioritize 20 percent of your main activities to achieve goals.
- Be accountable: Always schedule project deadline reminders earlier than anticipated so that you can deliver finished, quality products sooner than promised.
- Weekends. Don't work on Saturday or Sunday (or both, if possible).
- The Agenda. Always have an agenda for any meeting with two or more people to ensure all participants understand the meeting objectives.
- No interruptions: Manage controllable distractions.
- Plan things ahead: Dedicate at least 30 minutes a day to plan for tomorrow.
- Quick tasks list: Ponder tasks that you can complete in 5 minutes without much effort.
- Communication is everything: Make use of your quality resources and network to gather information quickly and complete tasks faster.
- Limit the number of daily tasks: Keep calm and keep things in perspective.
- Wake up early: Starting your day early gives you more time to plan and perform tasks.
- Delegate: If others can perform work better and faster than you, let them do it.

- Reduce travel time: Schedule web-based meetings and outsource your least favorite tasks.
- Grow openly: Even mistakes are opportunities to learn, grow, and perfect your skills.
- Community: Your business time is mainly about what problem you can solve for a community and long-term values you can deliver through your services or products. Take the time to make sure you are not losing focus on your community.
- Avoid small stuff: Too much time and energy is focused on the little things. Spend time on your vision, mission, and goals.
- Organize meetings ahead: Organized meetings help avoid wasting time on unimportant discussions.
- Rituals: Create a morning or evening ritual that benefits and motivates you to complete tasks based on the time of your highest energy levels.
- Time blocks: Finish work at a fixed time every day, and only emergencies should be considered outside the working time blocks.
- Collaborations and partnerships: Have a result in mind when collaborating with others to avoid wasting time communicating about trivialities while working on important and urgent project tasks.
- Opportunities: Consider only opportunities that help you make better decisions and choices that focus on your objectives and not someone else's.
- Vacations: These are meant to give you a break from work but also refresh your time perception and help you have a better perspective of the present and future situations.
- Celebrate achievements: Any achievement should be made public and accessible; documenting your journey will build your company timeline seamlessly.
- No procrastination: Start your planned projects quickly because procrastination is a thief of time.
- Supervise yourself: Conduct weekly time audits to determine the best strategies to maximize your time spent on income-generating activities.
- Track your day: Create a time log (or a to dos in your an calendar app) to track your daily time use.

- Morning priorities' review: If you did not get an opportunity to complete your to-do list last night, list your priorities for the day in the morning and determine what's essential and what's not crucial.
- Say *no* more often than you would: Make a *no* list of events or things that do not impact you, your business's bottom line, growth, and success.
- Find the best time blocks: Determine the time when you have the least interruptions.
- Important versus urgent priorities: Focus on accomplishing your top three primary goals and priorities weekly; define the difference between what you label as urgent versus critical.
- Rest is a valuable resource: Quality time is all about how you sleep, not how much you sleep.
- The power of habits: Convert the productive tasks you enjoy doing into practices; in the long run, it will make a huge difference.
- Resources: Do not become too dependent on third party resources; work on your own Wiki or resources list.
- Multitasking is an illusion: Recent psychological studies have shown that multitasking does not save time and yields less productivity, concentration, and focus.
- Workspace. Keep your workspace neat and organized.
- Build the right team. Collaborate with focused, like-minded professionals to grow your business and network.
- Write down your tasks and appointments: It is best to schedule events and meetings only on your calendar and use apps for other to-do items, tasks, notes, and reminders.
- Project management and time: Break your larger projects into small chunks ("time blocks"); build a team around people who believe in your vision with no expectations.
- Risk management. Schedule time for interruptions to allow yourself and your team to manage unplanned predicaments, or emergencies.
- Personal time. Create your own time by taking control of your schedule and categorize it to your preferences, not others.

CHAPTER 3

Time Flow

3.1 The Flow

Often, the reason why an idea is on your mind but seems impossible to deliver is that you want it to be different than it currently is.

That is why it's in your mind. Until all those thoughts have been explained and those choices made, and the resulting data has been kept in a system that you know you'll access and consider when you need to, your brain can't give up the task. You can fool everyone else, but you cannot trick your mind. Your mind knows whether or not you've come to the conclusions you need to and whether you've put the resulting outcomes and action reminders in a place within it that can be reliably accessed. If you have not done those things, it will not quit working overtime. Even if you have already decided on the next step, you will have to resolve an issue; your mind cannot go ahead until then. Moreover, if you do not park a reminder in a location it knows you will look, without fail, it will keep pressuring you about that untaken next thing, usually if you cannot do anything about it, which will only add to your anxiety.

At the very least, a portion of your mind is kind of stupid in an engaging manner. If it had some innate wisdom, it might remind you about the things you needed to perform only when you could do something about them. Do you have a flashlight somewhere with dead batteries in it? When does your mind tend to remind you that you need fresh batteries? When you observe the dead ones! That is not so smart. If your brain had any innate intelligence, it would remind you of those dead batteries only if you passed fresh ones at a store. And ones of the ideal dimensions, to boot.

The reason most coordinating systems have not worked for most people is they haven't yet transformed all of the stuff they are trying to organize. As long as it is still stuff, it is not controllable. Material planning is not necessarily a bad thing. But when we allow stuff to come into our personal and work lives, we've got an inherent commitment to ourselves to define and explain its significance. That's inherent in your work.If you did not have to consider those things, you are probably not required to. Furthermore, we will shortchange ourselves when we allow issues in our everyday lifestyle—home, family, health, finances, career, or relationships—to lie in our understanding because of a lack of significance of the particular outcomes and actions needed.

It's possible to train yourself, as an athlete, to be quicker, more responsive, more proactive, and more focused on dealing with all the things you need to take care of. You can minimize the ends across the entire range of your daily work life and private life and find a lot more done with less effort. And you can make front-end decisions about all the stuff you collect and create a standard operating procedure for working and living in this millennium.

What you can do with your time, what you can do with the information, and what you can do with your own body as well as your focus relative to your priorities, those are the real options to which you must allocate your limited resources. The substantive issue is how to make appropriate choices about what to do at any point in time. The real work will be to handle our actions. That may sound obvious. But it might amaze you to discover the number of next steps for the number of jobs and responsibilities remains undetermined by most people. It's tough to manage activities you have not identified or decided on. The majority of people have heaps of items that they need to do to make progress on several fronts, but they do not yet know what they are. The common complaint that "I don't have enough time to ____" (fill in the blank) is understandable because most projects seem overwhelming—and also, therefore, are overwhelming since you cannot plan at all! You may only do an action related to it.

I have discovered over the years the practical value of working on personal productivity improvement from the bottom up, beginning with the most mundane, ground-floor degree of current activity and commitments. Intellectually, the most suitable way should be to operate from the top down, first uncovering personal and organizational goals and vision, then defining critical objectives, and ultimately focusing on the particulars of implementation. The problem is, however, that many individuals are so embroiled in responsibilities on a day-to-day level, their ability to focus efficiently on the broader horizon is severely impaired. Consequently, a bottom-up strategy is usually more effective. Being up-to-date on, and also accountable for, what is in your in tray and on your mind at the moment, and incorporating practices that you can trust can help you remain this way, will offer the best means of broadening your horizons. A direct sense of freedom, release, and inspiration comes to individuals who roll their sleeves up and execute this process.

You'll be better equipped to tackle higher focused thinking as soon as your tools for handling the consequent actions for implementation are part of your continuing operational operational strategy. You will find more important things to consider than what is in your in tray, but if your management isn't as effective as it should be, it is like trying to swim in baggy clothes. Many executives I have worked with during the day to clean the decks of their mundane stuff have spent the day using a stream of ideas and visions about their organization and their future way of life. This happens as an automatic effect of unsticking their workflow.

You have to control obligations, projects, and activities in two ways—both vertically and horizontally. Horizontal control keeps coherence across all the tasks in which you are involved. Envision your mind continually scanning your environment like a police radar does; it may land on any of a million different items that invite or demand your attention during any 24-hour period: the pharmacy, your daughter's boyfriend, the board meeting, your aunt Martha, an incoming e-mail, the tactical plan, lunch, a wilting plant at the office, an upset customer, shoes that need polishing. You might be surprised by the number of items you think about and have to manage only in 1 day. You want an excellent system that could keep track of as many of these as possible, provide required information about them on demand, and allow you to change your attention from one thing to the next quickly and easily.

The goal for managing vertically and horizontally is the same: to put things off your head and have them done. Appropriate action direction allows you to feel comfortable and in control as you move through your broad spectrum of life and work. In contrast, proper project focusing makes you clear about and on course with the specifics needed.

The significant problem is that your brain keeps reminding you of matters when you cannot do anything about these. It does not have any sense of future or past. That means as soon as you tell yourself you might need to do something and store it just in your head, there's a part of you that believes you ought to be doing that something all the time. Whatever you have told yourself you ought to perform, it thinks you should do it at this time. Frankly, the moment you have two things to do stored only in your mind, you have generated private collapse since you cannot do them both at precisely the same time. This produces a pervasive stress factor whose origin cannot be pinpointed. The only time a lot of these will realize how much tension they have been under is to get rid of it and notice how different they behave. It is like the continuous buzzing noise you did not know was there in a room until it stops.

The psychology of time management relies on a straightforward principle called the Law of Control.

This legislation states that you truly feel good about yourself to the degree which you think you're in charge of your life. This legislation also means that you believe contrary to yourself to the degree to which you believe that you aren't in charge of your life or employment.

Psychologists refer to the difference between an inner locus of control, in which you think that you are the master of your destiny, along with an external locus of control, where you believe that circumstances outside yourself restrain you. Whenever you have an external locus of control, you think that you are commanded by your boss and your debts, and by the strain of your job and obligations. You believe you've too much to do in too little time and that you are not really in control of your time and your life. Most of what you are doing, hour after hour, is reacting and reacting to outside events. There is a difference between action that's self-determined and goal directed, and response, which can be a direct reaction to external stress. It's the difference between feeling positive and in control of your life and feeling bad, anxious, and pressured. To perform at your best, you must have a solid feeling of energy in the critical areas of your company and private life.

In psychological terms, each individual has a self-concept, an internal master program that modulates his behavior in every vital area of life. People with a high self-concept looking at time management see themselves and consider themselves as being well organized and effective. They are very much in control of their own lives and their job. Your self-concept is made up of all your ideas, images, pictures, and beliefs about yourself, particularly regarding how you handle your time.

Other folks feel continuously overwhelmed by the demands of other people and circumstances. What is your belief about your ability to manage your time?

Can you see yourself and believe about yourself as a highly efficient and effective time manager?

Can you think you are highly productive and in full control of your own life and work?

Whatever your belief, if you think of yourself as a superb time manager, you'll do the things that are consistent with this belief. Because your self-concept causes you to always strive for consistency between the person you find yourself as, on the interior, and the way you perform on the outside, if you believe you manage your time well, you'll be a good time manager. You may take all the classes on time management, read all the books, and practice the various systems, but if you perceive yourself as being a bad time manager, nothing will help. When you've developed the habit of being late for appointments and meetings, or you think that you are a disorganized person, these habits become your automatic behavior. If you do not change your beliefs about your degrees of efficiency and effectiveness, your ability to manage your time won't change either. Luckily, it is not tough. Most importantly, decide to develop a specific time direction addiction, like being early for every single meeting for the near future. Every shift in your life comes about when you make a definite, unequivocal decision to do something differently. Deciding to become a fantastic time supervisor is the first important step. As soon as you've decided to become an extremely productive person, there is a collection of personal programming methods that you could practice.

Step one is to change your inner dialogue. Ninety-five percent of your emotions, along with your planned activities, are determined by how you talk to yourself most of the time. Repeat to yourself, "I'm well organized and highly productive." Affirm over and over to yourself that "I am an excellent time manager." If people ask you about your time use, tell them, "I am an exceptional time manager." At any time you say, "I'm well organized," your subconscious accepts these phrases as a command and begins to motivate and drive you toward really becoming well organized in your behaviors. The next way to alter your behaviors is to picture yourself as an excellent time manager. See yourself as coordinated, effective, and in control of your own life. Bear in mind, the person you *see* on the interior is the person you will *be more* on the exterior. If you are already a well-organized and highly productive person, how do you act differently? What would differ from the way you behave today? Create a photo of yourself as calm, confident, highly efficient, more relaxed, and being able to complete considerable amounts of work in a short period. Imagine what a highly effective individual would look like.

Would the individual's desk be tidy and clean?

Would the individual look unhurried and unstressed?

Create a clear mental picture of yourself as someone who is in charge of his time and lifestyle. Think about yourself as being nicely organized in whatever you do. If you were excellent in time management, how do you act?

What would you be doing differently? About your time and personal productivity, what would be different from how you do things today?

Interestingly enough, even if you do not think that you are a good time supervisor now, but you pretend you already are, these activities will bring in the sense of personal efficiency. Since time direction is life management, improving your productivity starts with an evaluation of your values. It is not possible to manage your time properly unless you know just what your values are. Excellent time management expects that you bring your control over a sequence of events into harmony with what is most important to you. When it isn't essential to you, then you will never feel motivated and decide to have control over your time. Each individual has a profound need for purpose and meaning in life.

Among the substantial causes of personal tension and unhappiness is that what you're doing has no significance and purpose since it does not apply to you and your values and convictions. You'll be able to be effective with time management techniques, but it will not do you any good if you just become more skillful at doing something pointless for you. High efficiency will simply increase your sense of alienation, frustration, and stress. You may only feel pleased, valuable, and worthwhile to the level to which your day-to-day activities are in harmony with your values.

People who love what they do, and put their whole heart into their job since it's a reflection of their values, rarely experience anxiety or burnout of any sort. When you are living consistent with your values, you appear to experience a continuous flow of energy and productivity. Examine your values, your own innermost beliefs, and convictions and ask yourself what changes you could make to deliver your actions, on the outside, in alignment with your life priorities, on the inside. Time valuse emerge as a consequence of countless influences and experiences. They're a part of your emotional and psychological DNA. They're a part of your character and personality. They rarely change over time. Your job is to ascertain what your values are, then to arrange your life so that you are working and living consistently with these values. Frequently, you can end up working extremely hard at your work, but you haven't taken the time to stand back and think about exactly what it is you want to achieve.

Every time you ask and answer both of these questions, you will gain valuable insights that will allow you to look over your situation and know whether you are on the right path. As soon as you are clear about what you're trying to do and the way you are attempting to do it, you need to ask a third question: How is it moving? Is what you are doing toward what you want most quick and effective? What are your assumptions about your work and your life? What are your conscious assumptions? What are your unconscious and frequently unquestioned assumptions? It's impressive how many hardworking people are laboring predicated on false assumptions that they have never questioned. Many people are working hard but heading in the wrong direction, on the wrong path. They aren't clear about what they're attempting to do and where they would like to find themselves, but they do not want to confront or deal with the possibility that they might be incorrect. The procedure for asking tough questions necessitates *slow believing*, but it can significantly increase the speed at which you accomplish your business goals and your vision and mission. There are some areas of your job where slow believing is essential for you to perform at your very best. Take half an hour or more each day to review your goals, your plans, along with your progress. The ideal time to do that particular review is first thing in the morning. All exceptional executives and extremely efficient women and men set aside this time daily to carefully consider what they will do before they begin. You should read about, review, reflect on, and think about what you're doing before you take action. Over the years, I've read countless biographies and auto-biographies of women and men successful in various areas.

Just take the time to evaluate your own life and your actions in a broader context. Analyze the activities that you are engaged in now and determine which of them can have the most critical influence on your future. Then you come back to the present and make sure that everything you do at the moment is consistent with where you wish to be in the future. This is a highly effective technique that you may use too. Project forward, 2 or 3 years, and imagine your life situation is perfect whatsoever. From this vantage point of the future, look at yourself and describe your ideal life and work position. Ask yourself whether what you are doing is consistent with the development of your ideal future. Look at where you are today and see the steps that you will have to take to get to where you want to go. When you're clear about where you wish to be sometime in the future, it's far simpler for you to make better choices in the present. The principle is that long-term vision enhances short-term decision making. The custom of creating a longtime perspective is quite powerful. By projecting into the future and returning to the current, you may often see steps that you could take and errors that you could avoid. It will give you the emotional tools to arrange your time and actions to ensure what you are doing now is moving you toward introducing your ideal future. If you are not headed toward your destination, you do not want to get there any quicker. If you are not moving in your self-determined time management, then there is no purpose in handling your time in a manner that acceler-ates your rate of accomplishment. Time management plans and tactics applied without a clear vision of the future will get you to a destination that holds no interest for you, only quicker. As soon as you're clear about your values, vision, and mission for your life and work, and you're clear about exactly what it is you need to achieve and the best way to attain that, then and only then, can you start to apply some of the powerful time management techniques that are readily available to you. All suc-cessful time managers are useful planners. They make lists and sublists to achieve each significant and minor objective. Whenever a new job crosses their desk, they take the time to think through exactly what they want to achieve, and then write out an organized list, in sequence, of each step essential for this. Once you are clear about your goal, you make a list of everything you could imagine you will need to achieve that goal. Keep adding new things to the list because you think of these until your list is complete. Organize your listing in two ways: by importance and by priority. First, in coordinating by arrangement, you create a list of chronological order actions, from the first step to the final step before completion of the goal or endeavor. Second, you prioritize certain items, accepting that 20 percent of these items on your list will take time from the 80 percent of the crucial tasks in achieving your goal. Setting priorities permits you to stay focused on your critical tasks and actions without getting distracted. Review your plans regularly, particularly when you experience frustration or resistance of any kind. Be ready to update your plans when you receive new information or opinions. Remember that virtually every job has defects in it, both big and small. Continually seek out them. If you review your plans daily, you will get new insights about how to complete the task faster than you might have thought possible originally. Resist the temptation to take action before you've planned it out completely in advance. Perhaps the essential word related to achievement of any sort is *clarity*. Along with written goals, successful people have written strategies of action they follow every day. The most critical projects in the business and the persona time are finished by people who make comprehensive plans of activity before they start. Make composed plans for yourself and your company, and then follow these plans carefully till they succeed. Your ability to complete projects mostly determines your success in your career. A job is described as a *multitask job*. A job is an outcome that needs the conclusion of a string of numerous smaller jobs. A checklist consists of a set of written steps, in chronological order, that you create in advance of beginning work. Your ability to determine and specify the amounts for time that you will need to take you from where you are now to a finished project is a mark of exceptional thinking. The rule, once more, is that every minute spent in preparation and creating checklists will help save you 10 minutes in implementation and getting the job done. This is just another example of slow thinking that could significantly increase your effectiveness and your output, and your final value to your business. Produce a visual representation of your more significant tasks and jobs so that others and you might view them in their totality. Begin with the end in mind. Just take some time to create complete clarity about what your aims would seem like when they have been accomplished excellently. Make a list of the logical measures that you need to take to get from wherever you are to where you want to be. The superior executive presumes that there'll be problems, challenges, unexpected delays, and failures to complete the task by the agreed-on schedule. These happenings are a natural element of business life. You will achieve more with clear, written goals for each key person involved in the project than you could with great conversations and good intentions. Make goals clear, specific, quantifiable, and time bound. For each purpose or subgoal in the completion of a job or project, you have to assign responsibility to a specific person. Who will perform this task? When does the task need to be done, and to what type of quality? Never assume that people understand what you want unless you've made it apparent. The very amazing talent you have is your ability to behave, especially to think things through beforehand. The more time you take to think and plan on paper, the better results you will get, and the faster you can find those outcomes. All successful time managers think about paper and work out of a daily list of activities. The ideal time to create a record is the night before, which means that your subconscious mind can work on your record as you sleep. When you wake up in the morning, you may often have ideas and tips that will help you achieve some of the most crucial goals on your list. After each day, the last thing you do should be to plan out the next day; the ideal time control system that most of team driven business have found useful is a simple pad of paper where they wrote down everything they had to perform before they started. Many people toss and turn through the night, trying not to forget something they have to perform the next day. If you create a list before you go to sleep, writing down all you have planned for the upcoming workday, you will sleep far happier and awake more refreshed. Following time management experts, it takes about 12 minutes every day to compose a list of your tasks for this day. However, this record will save you ten times that several times in enhanced productivity. Twelve minutes spent preparing a daily list will provide you a revival of 120 minutes or 2 hours of increased productivity once you start work. That is an amazing payoff for such a simple task.

3.2   Habits

Active men and women establish good practices and make them their masters. Ineffective individuals accidentally develop poor habits, and then those bad habits govern their lives. Many men and women get into the practice of coming into work and immediately engaging in time-wasting, low-value or no-value pursuits. As soon as they arrive, they find someone to talk to, read the newspaper, assess their e-mail, get a cup of coffee, and generally begin coasting through the day. But whatever you do daily becomes a habit. Unfortunately, the vast majority of individuals at work today have established the practice of wasting the majority of their time on activities that bring nothing to their own companies or their professions. They get comfortable doing certain activities in a certain way. Even after they've been encouraged to higher level responsibilities, they always slip back into doing things that are no longer mandatory or that other people could do equally well, or even better. Never do anything that's not on your list. If a new task or job comes up, write it down in your list and specify a priority for this before you begin work on it.

Any time management system is far better than no time control system in any way. There are lots of smartphone apps that will help you manage your time. There are time management software and apps that you can install on your computer. You can use a composed time management system that you maintain with your notes and update frequently. Just keep in mind that in the area of work, the only thing you need to sell is time. Be certain that you are focusing your time on the most valuable and foremost things that you can do to create the most significant contribution for your company. Just as you need a to-do listing to guide you through a hectic day, you want a not-to-do listing to keep you on track. These are things that you decide, in advance, that you're not going to do, no matter how tempting they may be if they come up. Bear in mind, you may just get your time if you stop doing things of reduced value. You already have significantly more work than you may ever get done.

You will never get caught up in your existing tasks and responsibilities if you have a clear and defined series of priorities and mental checkboxes in your time management strategy.

Instead, say no. In technically no time, you will have your time entirely under your control.

Each of the time management strategies boils down to helping you decide the most crucial task you can do in the present time and giving you the tools and techniques to start immediately with that one task, which means it is possible to keep working on it it is complete. As it is the most critical question in each time direction, ask yourself repeatedly where you should put your time resources until it becomes an automatic pattern that inspires and drives you to concentrate on your highest value task or activity. When you arrange all of your time and work tasks around the answer to this query, you will be astonished at how much more effective you become and how quickly. Every task that you work on brings a value of some sort, either low or high. Your work is to concentrate on the most valuable use of your time and to subject yourself to constantly work on those few activities that contribute the most important value to your job and your company. This focus on the most valuable use of your time could be applied to every area of your life. Sometimes, the most valuable use of time is to spend it face-to-face with the indispensable people in your life. At other times, the most valuable use of your time is to read a fantastic book rather than watch television. Regarding your tasks and activities, setting priorities is mostly about separating the *vital few* from the *trivial many*. There are four distinct kinds of tasks that you're faced with every-day. Your capacity to sort out these tasks into their proper categories can significantly boost your productivity. Each of these tasks can be placed in a different quadrant or box. A significant task is something that has long-term consequences for your livelihood. An urgent task is something that cannot be delayed or put off. A job that is both urgent and important is something that is *in your face*. It is primarily determined by outside demands on your time, responsibilities, and duties; it is something that you must start and finish to maintain on top of your work. You will find people you need to scrutinize, tasks you have to review, and places you need to go to. You will find clients to meet, tasks to finish, and activi-ties that others expect you to perform. Most people spend most of their working day on jobs that are equally urgent and crucial. The other sort of jobs are those that are important but not urgent. They can be delayed or procrastinated upon, at least for the short term. An example of a job that's vital but not urgent is a critical report that you must have written, approved, and filed by the close of the month. Or consider a school term paper. It's critical to your grade at the end of the semester, but it is also something that may be put off for months and weeks, and frequently is. Throughout your life, you're surrounded by essential but not urgent tasks. Reading crucial publications in your area, taking extra courses, updating your skills are all vital to your long-term success, but they are not urgent. Thus, you procrastinate doing them. Most people who fail or underachieve in business have sadly put off updating their skills for so long that they are simply passed and surpassed by other, more determined and aggressive people who want to enjoy greater rewards. Even something as straightforward as physical exercise is vital to your health, but not urgent. It is possible to set it off for a protracted duration, and the majority of people do. You probably have people coming to your workplace, texting or calling you, sending you e-mails. However, your answers to them donate little or no value to your enterprise or your job. Many people invest as much as half of the time engaging in actions that are urgent but not important. They're fun, simple, and enjoyable, but they do not lead to work at all. The majority of activities that involve an unplanned conversation with colleagues or low-value/no-value events are not urgent, as productive communication is always linked to a defined meeting plan and can be easily summarized in series of bullet points. The fourth type of action that people engage in at the workplace are the jobs that are neither urgent nor important. A lot of men and women participate in activities that have zero significance to themselves or the corporation. The key to proper time management is for you to set priorities and constantly to be working on what is both urgent and essential, that is, your most pressing and crucial tasks. Once you are through with your work that is urgent and important, you immediately start work on those tasks that are important but not urgent at the moment. The functions that are important but not urgent are usually those activities and actions that could enhance to your livelihood in a meaningful manner in the long term.

3.3   Focus

Developing absolute clarity regarding your key result areas is essential for your efficacy and higher productivity. Your key result areas are those things you have been hired to perform, accomplish, or reach. They are your top priorities in terms of the value that you contribute to your enterprise. These are the tasks that, once performed, determine whether or not you fulfill your responsibilities to your company as well as to yourself. In your job, you will find things that only you can perform. If you don't do them, nobody else will do them for you. If you do them nicely, it will create an extraordinary difference in your project and your business. All high time-demanding activities that contribute to the highest value to your job should always be planned. To perform at the maximum level, you must be clear about what those actions are, which are more valuable than any other people, and which only you can perform to distinction. Focusing on key outcome areas is the most direct approach to unleash effectiveness, energy, persuasion, excitement, and vitality. On the other hand, in the age of diversion, you experience feelings of reduced self-esteem, frustration, stress, and often depression when you're doing something that, you know, makes little difference to attaining your major objectives. Everyone at every level of the company should know what his or her significant results are. Make certain all workers who report to you are clear about the most valuable contribution that they can make to your organization. One of the greatest kindnesses that you can give to those who report to you is to help them become crystal clear about the precious and foremost things they can perform and assist them in achieving those goals in time. If you do not understand the answers to these questions, you cannot assist your boss get his or her occupation, which is very important to your success. What's more, each individual who reports to you must know the answer to this query about you as well. Your understanding of how to properly delegate lower value tasks to others who can do them at a lesser hourly rate or salary is among those vital skills of contemporary management. Delegate anything you know doesn't require your immediate attention to others who can perform the tasks in addition to or better than you. If someone else can perform a particular task 70 percent as well as you, this task is a prime candidate for you to get off your plate and onto that person's plate. Delegation enables you to progress from what you can do personally to everything you can manage. Delegation is the skill that allows you to leverage your skills and expertise and multiply them multiple times throughout all the colleagues who can be given small tasks linked to the same job. You always have an option. You might also delegate problem solving and decision making if they are among your duties and obligations. It's possible to transfer information gathering and analysis. You can delegate every task that anybody else can do as well as (or almost as well as) you. With the art of delegation, which is easily learnable, your limitations at work will reduce. You are not going to end up doing things of low value or no value. Focus means that once you start on your most important task, you resolve to persevere without distraction or diversion. Your ability to concentrate single-mindedly on the most important use of your time would be the number one necessity for success. You could meet each other's needs with intelligence, experience, and imagination, but if you cannot focus on one thing at one time, then you cannot progress. If you do not discipline yourself to focus single-mindedly, you will invariably end up working on low-priority jobs. Single handling is among the most crucial of all time management methods and life management principles.

As soon as you start a task, you stay with it until it's 100 percent complete. Apply single handling to your email and other documents. Deselect unnecessary items instantly and then deal with the vital documents just once, either by filing or responding to them right away. Single handling can lessen the time spent completing an essential job by as much as 80 percent, and dramatically increase the quality of the finished work. There is a great deal of debate today over the notion of multitasking. When you return to the previous occupation, you're merely making a shift of attention, like pointing a light beam from one goal to another. Following that, you must speed up on the job before getting started again on a new series of tasks. Multitasking is tempting. However, it is an insidious use of time. It can sabotage your career and undermine your ability to achieve the vital tasks upon which all your success depends. You require a minimum of 60 to 90 minutes to accomplish anything worthwhile. It takes about 30 minutes simply to get your mind into a complex endeavor, like preparing a proposal, report, or perhaps planning an important project. Once you are single-minded, focus on the task; you can then concentrate single-mindedly at a high degree of awareness and imagination for another 60 minutes or more on intense work. You can't mix creative jobs with functional or administrative jobs. You cannot do operational tasks and creative jobs concurrently. Office activities need quick, short-term execution. Creative jobs require thought, plans, and programs. First, operate in the morning when you are the freshest and most alert. Even if you get into the office a bit overdue, in these 90 minutes of uninterrupted work, you will accomplish as much as the average man does in a workplace environment in 3 hours. Another time that you can use to your advantage is lunchtime. This is an excellent chance for you to shut off your phone, switch off your Internet link, and eliminate other distractions while everybody else is out of the office having lunch. You'll have 60 straight minutes of peace where you can do the job single-mindedly to clean up some of your most essential tasks. Another strategy you can use would be to shut your office door for specific intervals every day, during which you work single-mindedly on your most significant tasks. Everyone knows that while this sign is about the door, no one is permitted to disrupt except in the event of a true emergency. It ends up that individuals are the most important time wasters from the world of work. Many people come into action in the morning, begin chitchatting with their colleagues, and then continue for another 2 or 3 hours working to take random breaks in between tasks. When you go into your workplace, start work immediately. Do not talk with other people, read the newspaper, or browse the Internet. Since you planned your day out the day before, you begin immediately on your main endeavor and keep functioning, task by task, until you get your most important jobs done. When you complete a collection of similar or identical tasks at a row, then the learning curve allows you to decrease the time necessary to finish each activity by up to 80 percent from the time you finish the 5th identical task. By way of example, in writing letters or replying to e-mail, you bundle them all together and perform them at the same time. If you need to interview several individuals, speak with them, one after another. *Do all of your similar jobs at precisely the same time* rather than doing a little bit now and a little bit later. Also, how you deal with your e-mail is going to have an important impact on your livelihood. Some people are slaves for their e-mail. They have a bell that goes off each time a new e-mail comes in, and leaving anything they are doing, they flip instantly to their inbox to check the message. To achieve maximum productivity, then you have to set the telephone in its place so that you do not find yourself a slave to anyone who dials the number. The best way to get control over your phone calls would be to get all of them screened by your administrative assistant; alternatively, put your phone on silent and allow calls to go to your voicemail. There are just a few messages or calls that may not wait till it's more convenient for you to turn your focus to dealing with them. *One of the reasons that we are becoming slaves to the appeal of diversion is interest.* We can't stop ourselves from wondering who is sending us a message or who is on the opposite end of the telephone. The only way to resist this temptation to be diverted is for you to switch off the phone completely so that you don't even listen to it ring. Whenever you meet your employees and assistants or with your boss or with customers, have your requirements ready for review. Permit no interruptions whatsoever. There's seldom anything so significant that it can't wait. Ten minutes of uninterrupted time in conversation with another person will be more productive than 30 or 40 minutes with the phone ringing and answered during your discussion. It is possible to call people back, one after another. If it is an urgent telephone, write out your schedule for the call, so you are working from a list when you're talking to another person.

There are few things as exasperating as getting off a critical phone call with a difficult-to-reach person and finding that you have forgotten to convey an important point because you didn't write it down. Establish telephone appointments precisely as you would establish a face-to-face meeting in the workplace. When you have a meeting call, leave a particular time to be accessible after the meeting has happened. If team members call you, and you cannot talk with them, have your assistant or chat bot get a call-back time that's convenient for the caller. It should be through hours when you'll be at your workplace or available by telephone so that you can return calls on time. Use the telephone as a business tool.

Get straight to the point. Be considerate and friendly, however, businesslike and result oriented. The more precise and prepared you can be on the time and content of your telephone conversation, the more you'll get done quicker, and the more productive you'll be in each telephone call. Be certain that you have a good reason for calling or calling any meeting.

Look upon each session as a business investment.

Look upon a meeting as carrying a price in staff and managerial time and wages.

Simply take the joint hourly pay of those folks in those meetings and realize that you have to have a return on your investment of the sum of money. Avoid unnecessary meetings.

Always ask whether that meeting has to be held in any way. Every time a meeting is useless, it's necessary not to have a meeting. If you don't need to attend the assembly, then do not visit. If you're organizing the conference, ask yourself who's vital to it, and invite those individuals. Refrain from inviting individuals who don't have to be there simply in order to make them feel good or exceptional. Prepare an agenda for each meeting, and always follow a written schedule. Prioritize the items on the agenda and deal with the main ones first in case you run out of time.

If you have those who are chronically late, you could consider locking the door soon after your start time. Another strategy is to assume that the latecomer is not coming at all and start the meeting. Once the session begins, ensure that there'll be no interruptions while you're at the conference. Request more questions and listen closely than you talk or contribute to the agenda. Utilize a meeting to elicit the very best thinking of every individual in the room, which is not possible if you are talking all the time. To succeed today, you have to stay current with your research prerequisites. We reside in a knowledge-based society, and one key item of data can have an immediate result on your work and your decision making. Just take some time to become discerning about what you read. Resist the temptation to spend time studying things that are not of immediate value or relevance to your life and work. You cannot avoid all of the incoming information, but you can sort it and go through it in a time and context that make sense to you. If you have not ever taken a course in speed-reading, then you should do it now. This will let you double your reading speed and degree of retention, likely from the first two classes. Self-development must be an ongoing and continuous part of the time used daily. It is a crucial time management purpose that can place you on the path to the executive suite and beyond. Locate the time in your program to keep on growing and growing. The fundamental rule about personal advancement is that you can go no further than you have gone now with your existing knowledge and skill. To advance your career, you need to obtain more expertise. You have to learn more to earn more. Work on improving and developing yourself daily. If you read something for 1 hour each day that enhances your ability to do your job, that would put you in the top 1 percent in our society within five decades. Review all of your notes, emails and to dos from the appropriate documents, both physical and online. Deal only with your current endeavor. Try to have just one item before you whenever possible. The top professionals in every field keep a tidy and highly organized workspace at all times. Many people believe they work more efficiently in a messy work environment, using a cluttered desk. Yet every study that's been done with individuals shows that when they're made to clean up their work environment, so they have just one job facing them, their productivity doubles and triples, normally overnight. Individuals working with cluttered desks can be found to devote an enormous amount of each working day searching for the substances they want among the clutter around them.

The most significant thing you could instill in your own life is balance and moderation. By practicing the ideas and methods in this book, you will get a master time supervisor and have more time for your family and your private life. Often, individuals take time management programs so that they can increase the number of things that they can perform on an everyday basis. The primary intention of learning and practicing time management skills is to improve and improve the overall quality of your life. It's to grow the quantity of pleasure you encounter.

A wonderful life is one that is in equilibrium. Should you spend sufficient time preserving and enhancing the quality of your relationships, you will find that you get more joy, satisfaction, and fulfillment out of your job; you will find success.

CHAPTER 4

Time and Project Management

4.1 Environment

If your space is correctly set up and compact, it can reduce your unconscious resistance to dealing with your stuff and also make it attractive for you to sit down and crank through your input and your work. A perfect period for most people is two whole days, back to back. (Don't be put off by that if you do not have that long to spend, however. Doing some of the activities I suggest will be useful, however much or how little time you devote to them. Two days aren't required to benefit from such techniques and principles— they will begin to pay off almost immediately.) Implementing the complete workflow can take up to 6 hours or longer, and clarifying and deciding on activities for all of the input you'll want to externalize and capture in your system can easily take another 8 hours. Of course, you can even collect and process your items in balls, but it'll be a lot easier if you can handle that front-end portion in one fell swoop. The perfect time for me to work with someone in executing this methodology is on a weekend or vacation because the chance of outside disturbance is minimal then.

You'll have to opt for a physical place to serve as your central cockpit of control. If you already have an office and a desk area set up where you work, that's possibly the best place to get started. If you operate from a home office, that will be your prime location. , You'll want to set up identical, even interchangeable, systems in the working area; however, one will most likely be primary. Should you feel you don't have either—you don't have some central physical spot you'd call home for dealing with your stuff—you must create one. Even if you have a portable, high-tech lifestyle that's mainly virtual, you will still require a private setting for a base camp from which to operate. You will want to implement this program to do work and procedure input signal, but beginning with a primary location is best. The workspace principles are just a writing surface and room for an in tray, and likely (for many people) space for center electronics. Some, such as a foreman in a machine shop, an intake nurse on a hospital floor, or your children's nanny, will not need a whole lot more than that. Many homemakers will not necessarily need a vast region to manage their workflow. Still, with enough of a discrete space dedicated to the processing of notes, e-mail, household tasks, financing, are critical.

A functional workspace is crucial. If you do not already have a dedicated workspace and in tray, get them today. Everybody must have a physical locus of control from where to deal with everything else.

Do not skimp on the workspace at home. As you'll discover utilizing this process, you must have at least a satellite home system similar to a mobile office with the essential tools necessary to achieve any urgent task.

If you move around considerably, as a business traveler or just as a person with a mobile lifestyle, you will also want to set up an efficiently organized micro-office-in-transit. More than likely, this will consist of a briefcase, package, or satchel with proper folders and portable workstation supplies. A lot of men and women lose chances to become productive because they're not equipped to make the most of their odd windows and moments that open up as they move from one spot to another, or when they are in off-site environments. The combination of a fantastic processing fashion, proper tools, and interconnected work systems at home and work may make travel a highly leveraged way to get certain kinds of jobs done. As technology continues to provide both more powerful mobile hardware and quick global access to most of us, the ability to manage our life virtually increases.

You may work almost anywhere if you've got a clean, compact system and also understand how to process your stuff quickly and portably. But you'll still need a house base using a well-grooved set of tools and sufficient space for all the reference and support team that you will want somewhere close at hand when you land. Most of the people I work with demand at least two file drawers because of their general reference and project support kinds of paper-based materials. Given digital scanners, along with the continual technological improvements in this regard, it is conceivable that one day all that service substance can be in the cloud and retrievable as necessary, anywhere. Any device that can convert an offline physical document into a digital file is undoubtedly a vital element in handling particular sorts of information and reminders of the responsibilities and knowledge that relate to specific times and days. If there are numerous reminders and a few data, you will need a calendar. Still, you won't be stopping there: Your schedule will need to be integrated with a far more comprehensive system that will appear as you apply this method.

A straightforward and extremely functional personal reference system is essential to this procedure. The filing system is one of the first things I assess before starting the workflow process in anyone's office.

A random nonactionable but possibly relevant material, unprocessed and unorganized, produces a debilitating psychological sound. More importantly, it provides a block at the *leak* part of a workflow, and things tend to back up into the region, as we see in clogged plumbing. Many times I have pushed to the local office supply store with a client and bought a filing cabinet, a big pile of file folders, along with a labeler, so we could make an appropriate place to place two-thirds of the material lying around his or her office and desk. The transformation in clarity and focus regarding work was necessarily striking. If you are a digitally oriented person, you might think there is no longer any need for document folders.

I strongly suggest that you keep up a private, at-hand submitting system—both physical and digital. It should take less than 1 minute to pick something up from your in tray or print it from an e-mail, decide it needs no next action, but has some possible future value, and finish keeping it in a trusted system. The same is true for scanning and saving documents or copying and pasting data in the computer. You may have a preponderance of digital over paper-based reference material (or vice versa). Still, without a streamlined system for both, you will resist keeping potentially invaluable information or that which you do keep will collect in inappropriate places. If it takes longer than a minute to document something in an easily retrievable format, then you will need a pro to stack it or stuff it somewhere rather. Besides being fast, the system needs to be fun and easy, current, and complete. Otherwise, you will unconsciously resist draining your in tray because you know there's very likely to be something in there that should get registered. .The electronic world provides the benefit of the search function over a broad swath of your data. The ability to tag content with keywords adds even more capability for retrieval. However, with so many options and options to have various storage locations, information can also quickly increase in complexity and confuse retrieval. Most of the people I know who are even moderately busy will not take the time and attempt to utilize these tools to catalog all their stuff within all their potential applications. So, although the computer gives us great flexibility and power and opportunity for a vast reference library, it generates an even more significant challenge to design your own natural and practical formats for referential information. Even digitally, it's beneficial to have a visual map sorted in ways that make sense—either by indexes or information, collections arranged efficiently, usually in an alpha format. The biggest issue for digitally oriented folks is that the simplicity of storing and capturing has generated a write-only syndrome: All they're doing is obtaining information—not actually accessing and using it intelligently. Some understanding needs to be applied to keep one's possibly vast digital library functional versus a black hole of data readily dumped in there with a couple of keystrokes.

Wherever things of different personalities or significance are piled into the same location, it's too much work to continually think about the nature of these contents, which means that your brain will go numb to the pile.

Reference materials need to be contained and organized in their discrete boundaries—digitally and physically—so that they don't cloud other categories in the human body, are available for a specific purpose, and can be obtained efficiently. Since they can be so voluminous, it is critical that they're easily handled for finding, sorting, and accessing what you need, when you require it, and that they don't get in the way of their action-oriented components of your machine.

4.2   A Quick Overview on Scrum

Scrum is based on an empirical process control concept. Three pillars uphold every execution of effective process control: transparency, inspection, and adaptation. Significant aspects of the procedure have to be visible to those accountable for the outcome. Transparency requires those aspects to be defined by a common standard, so observers share a common understanding of what's being seen. Their inspection shouldn't be so frequent that control gets in the way of their job.

Reviews would be most beneficial when diligently performed by skilled inspectors at the point of activity. If an inspector determines that one or more facets of a process deviate outside acceptable limits and that the resulting product will be unsatisfying, the process or the material being processed must be adjusted. An adjustment must be made whenever possible to minimize further deviation. The Scrum Team includes a Product Owner, the Development Team, and a Scrum Master. Scrum Teams are self-organizing and cross-functional.

The group model in Scrum is intended to maximize flexibility, creativity, and productivity. Incremental deliveries of *done* products ensure a possibly useful version of a functioning product is always available. How this is done may vary across organizations, Scrum Teams, and individuals. The Product Owner is the only person responsible for handling the Product Backlog. Product Backlog management comprises the following:

1. Clearly expressing Product Backlog items
2. Ordering the items in the Product Backlog to achieve best results
3. Optimizing the work the Development Team performs
4. Ensuring that the Product Backlog is visible and clear to all, and reveals what the Scrum Team can be used forEnsuring the Development Team understands items in the Product Backlog

The Product Owner may do the aforementioned work, or have the Development Team do it; however, the Product Owner remains accountable.

For the Product Owner to succeed, the whole organization must respect its decisions. The Product Owner's choices are observable in the ordering and content of the Product Backlog. Nobody is permitted to inform the Development Team to operate from a different set of requirements, and the Development Team isn't authorized to act on what anybody else says.

The Development Team consists of professionals who do the job of delivering a potentially releasable increment of a *done* product at the end of each Sprint.

Development Teams are structured and enabled by the organization to organize and manage their job. Development Teams have the following attributes:

1. They're self-organizing. They are cross-functional, with all the skills as a team necessary to create a product increment.
2. Scrum recognizes no titles for Development Team members other than Developer, no matter the work being done by the person; there are no exceptions to this rule.
3. Scrum recognizes no subteams from the Development Team, regardless of particular domain names that need to be addressed, like testing or business analysis.
4. Individual Development Team members may have technical skills and areas of focus, but accountability is owned by the Development Team as a whole.

Optimal Development Team size is small enough to stay nimble and big enough to complete considerable work within a Sprint. More than three Development Team members reduces interaction and leads to lower productivity gains.

Smaller Development Teams may experience skill constraints during the Sprint, making the team unable to deliver a potentially releasable increment.

Large Development Teams create too much complexity for an experimental process to be managed. The Product Owner and Scrum Master roles are not included in this count unless they are also executing the job of the Sprint Backlog.

Scrum Masters do it by ensuring that the Scrum Team adheres to Scrum theory, practices, and principles. The Scrum Master helps the organization understand which of the interactions with the Scrum Team are useful and which aren't. The Scrum Master helps everyone alter these connections to maximize the value created by the Scrum Team. The Scrum Master helps the Product Owner in several ways, such as the following:

1. Locating techniques for successful Product Backlog management
2. Helping the Scrum Team understand the need for clear and concise Product Backlog items

3. Understanding product preparation in an empirical surrounding
4. Ensuring the Product Owner knows how to organize the Product Backlog to maximize value
5. Understanding and practicing agility
6. Facilitating Scrum occasions as requested or needed

The Scrum Master serves the Development Team in several ways, such as the following:

1. Training the Development Team at self-organization and cross-functionality
2. Helping the Development Team to make high-value products
3. Eliminating impediments to the Development Team's progress
4. Facilitating Scrum occasions as needed or requested
5. Coaching the Development Team in organizational environments in which Scrum is not yet fully adopted and known

The Scrum Master serves the business in several ways, including the following:

1. Leading and training the organization in its Scrum adoption
2. Planning Scrum implementations inside the organization
3. Helping employees and stakeholders understand and enact Scrum product development
4. Causing change that increases the productivity of the Scrum Team
5. Working with other Scrum Masters to increase the effectiveness of the application of Scrum in the organization (Prescribed events are used in Scrum to create regularity and to minimize the need for meetings not defined in Scrum.)

All events are time-boxed occasions, such that every event has a maximum duration. Once a Sprint starts, its length is fixed and cannot be shortened or lengthened. The rest of the functions may end whenever the purpose of the event is accomplished, ensuring an appropriate amount of time is spent without permitting waste in the process. Aside from the Sprint itself, which is a container for all other events, each event in Scrum is an official opportunity to inspect and adapt something. Failure to include any of these events results in decreased clarity and is a lost opportunity to inspect and adapt.

When a Sprint's horizon is too long, the definition of what's being constructed may change, complexity may rise, and risk could increase. Sprints enable predictability by ensuring review and adaptation of progress toward a Sprint Goal at least each calendar month. Sprints also limit risk to a calendar month of price. Only the Product Owner has the authority to cancel the Sprint, although he or she may do this under the influence of the stakeholders, the Development Team, or the Scrum Master. A Sprint is going to be canceled if the Sprint Goal becomes obsolete. This could occur if the company changes direction or if the industry or technology conditions change. In general, a Sprint should be canceled if it no longer makes sense, given the circumstances. But, because of the short duration of Sprints, cancelation rarely makes sense.

The job done on them depreciates quickly and must be regularly reestimated. Sprint cancelations consume resources because everyone has to regroup in a different Sprint Planning to begin another Sprint. Sprint cancelations are very unusual. The work to be performed from the Sprint is planned at the Sprint Planning.

Sprint Planning is time boxed to a maximum of 8 to 10 hours to get a 1-month Sprint. For shorter Sprints, the event is usually quicker. The Scrum Master ensures that the event takes place and that attendants understand its purpose.

The Scrum Master teaches the Scrum Team to keep planning inside the agreed timebox.

Scenario 1

The Development Team works to forecast the functionality that will be developed during the Sprint.

The Product Owner discusses the objective that the Sprint should achieve and the Product Backlog items, which, if completed in the Sprint, would satisfy the Sprint Goal.Only the Development Team can assess what it can accomplish over the forthcoming Sprint. The Sprint Goal is a goal that will be fulfilled within the Sprint throughout the implementation of the Product Backlog, and it provides advice to the Development Team on why it's building the increment.

Scenario 2

Having set the Sprint Goal and selected the Product Backlog items for the Sprint, the Development Team determines how it will make this functionality into a *done* stock increment during the Sprint.

Work may be of varying sizes or estimated effort. But enough work is planned during Sprint Planning for the Development Team to forecast what it believes it can do in the upcoming Sprint. Work designed for the first days of the Sprint by the Development Team is decomposed by the end of the meeting, frequently into units of 1 day or less. The Development Team self-organizes to undertake the job in the Sprint Backlog, both during Sprint Planning and as needed throughout the Sprint.

From the end of the Sprint Planning, the Development Team should be able to describe to the Product Owner and Scrum Master how it intends to work as a self-organizing team to achieve the Sprint Goal and make the required increment.

The Sprint Goal is a goal set for the Sprint that can be met through the implementation of the Product Backlog. It guides the Development Team on why it's building the increment. It's made during the Sprint Planning meeting. The Sprint Goal provides the Development Team some flexibility over the functionality implemented inside the Sprint.

The Sprint Goal can be another coherence that causes the Development Team to work together instead of on separate initiatives. As the Development Team functions, it retains the Sprint Goal in mind. To fulfill the Sprint Goal, it implements functionality and technology. The Daily Scrum is a 15-minute time-boxed occasion for the Development Team to synchronize activities and make a plan for the next 24 hours. This is done by inspecting the job since the last Daily Scrum and forecasting the job that could be done before the next one. The Daily Scrum is held at the same time and place every day to reduce complexity. The Development Team utilizes the Daily Scrum to inspect progress toward the Sprint Goal and to inspect the way that growth is trending toward completing the work in the Sprint Backlog. The Daily Scrum optimizes the probability that the Development Team will meet the Sprint Goal. Every day, the Development Team should understand how it intends to work together as a self-organizing team to accomplish the Sprint Goal and create the anticipated increment by the end of the Sprint. The Development Team or team members often meet immediately after the Daily Scrum for detailed discussions, or to adapt or replan the remainder of the Sprint's work. The Scrum Master teaches the Development Team to keep the Daily Scrum inside the 15-minute time box. The Scrum Master enforces the principle that only Development Team members participate in the Daily Scrum. Daily Scrums enhance communications, remove additional meetings, identify impediments to development for removal, highlight and encourage quick decision making, and improve the Development Team's level of knowledge. This is a key to inspect and adapt to the assembly. A Sprint Review is held after the Sprint to check the increment and accommodate the Product Backlog if needed. Based on this and any changes to the Product Backlog during the Sprint, attendees work on the upcoming things that could be done to optimize value.

The Sprint Retrospective is an opportunity for the Scrum Team to inspect itself and create a strategy for improvements to be enacted during the next Sprint. The Sprint Retrospective happens after the Sprint Review and before another Sprint Planning. This is a 3-hour time-boxed assembly for 1-month Sprints. For shorter Sprints, the event is generally quicker. The Scrum Master participates as a peer team member in the meeting from the accountability over the Scrum process. By the end of the Sprint Retrospective, the Scrum Team must have identified improvements that will help in the next Sprint. When a Product Backlog item is described as *done*, everybody must understand what *done* means.

Although improvements might be performed at any time, the Sprint Retrospective provides a formal opportunity to concentrate on control and adaptation. Scrum depends on transparency. Decisions to optimize value and control risk are created based on the perceived condition of the artifacts. To the extent that transparency is achieved, these choices have a sound basis. To the extent that the items are incompletely transparent, these choices can be flawed, the value may diminish, and risk may increase. A Scrum Master can detect sketchy slides by inspecting the artifacts, sensing patterns, listening attentively to what is being said, and discovering differences between expected and real results.

The identical description guides the Development Team in understanding how many Product Backlog items it can select during a Sprint

Planning. Development Teams provide an increment of product performance every Sprint. The purpose of each Sprint is to deliver increments of deployable functionalities. If *done* for an increment isn't a convention of the development organization, the Development Team of the Scrum Team must specify a definition of *done* suitable for the item. If multiple Scrum Teams are working on the product or system release, the Development Teams on each of the Scrum Teams must mutually define *Done*. Since Scrum Teams mature, it is expected that their definitions of *Done* will expand to include more stringent standards for higher quality.

4.3   Beyond the Scrum of Scrums

Let us take into consideration the following scenario: You are managing a software development team where there is a high percentage of innovation, creativity, or testing required. You need to build or expand systems, which allow partitioning of work, with clean interfacing, components, or objects. You want to make sure you are weighing the needs of developers to work undisturbed and the requirement for management and the customer to see real progress.

A list of points to check before defining Sprints can be:

- Overhead is made to determine that a procedure is on track.
- Often, by the time systems are addressed, they are obsolete or need significant changes. The challenge is that resulting input from the environment is accumulated mostly at the start of the project, while the user mostly achieves the system or intermediate releases.
- It is often assumed that a development procedure is a well-understood approach that is planned and estimated. If a project fails, that is considered evidence that the development process needs more rigor. These step-by-step methods, however, do not work because they do not cope with the unpredictable issues, both human and technical, in system administration. At the beginning of a project, it is impossible to generate a complete, detailed plan because of the many uncertainties involved.
- Developers need time to work uninterrupted, but they need support for logistics; management and users need to be convinced that real progress is being made.

Divide the job in Sprints. A Sprint is approximately 30 days, where an agreed quantity of work will be conducted to create a deliverable. Each Sprint takes a preallocated amount of work from the Backlog, and it is assigned to Sprints by priority and by a likeness of what could be achieved through the Sprint's length. Undisturbed by outside interruptions, you are free to adapt your ways of working with insights and opportunities.

The goal of a Sprint would be to complete as much excellent software as possible and to ensure real progress, not newspaper milestones as alibis. Sprints are quick; as a result, the issue of completing a Sprint is much simpler than that of completing a project. It is a lot easier to take up this smaller challenge. The end users are intensely involved during the development of the application through the Demos following the Sprints. However, they are not allowed to interfere with daily activities. Project status is observable since the Sprint produces working code. What is the best way to arrange the work to be done next and at any stage of the project? The Backlog is the job to be delivered on an item. The accomplishment of this work will transform the product from its current form into its vision. However, in Scrum, the Backlog evolves as the product, and the context in which it will be used evolves. The Backlog is dynamic, changed continuously by management to ensure that the product defined by completing the Backlog is the most suitable, aggressive, useful product potential. There are many resources for the Backlog list. Item marketing adds work that will fulfill their vision of the goods. Technology adds work that will ensure the product uses the most innovative and productive technology. The development adds work to boost product functions. Customer support adds work to fix underlying product flaws. Only one person prioritizes work. This man is responsible for fulfilling the product vision. The title usually is product manager or product marketing manager. If anyone needs the priority for work changed, they must convince this man to change this priority.

The highest priority, Backlog, has the maximum definition. Additionally, it is prioritized with an eye toward dependencies. Depending on how quickly products are required in the marketplace and the financing of the organization, one or more Scrum Teams work on a product's Backlog. As a Scrum Team is ready (newly formed or just finished a Sprint) to work on the Backlog, the team meets with the item manager. In doing so, the Scrum

Team may change the Backlog priority by choosing a Backlog that is mutually supportive, that is, one that can be worked on at once more quickly than by waiting. Examples are multiple work items that require developing a standard module or interface, which makes sense to add in one Sprint. The group selects a cohesive group of high-priority Backlog things that, once completed, will have attained an objective or a landmark. This is said as Sprint's objective. During the Sprint, the team is free not to do work as long as this objective is attained. The group now decomposes the selected Backlog into tasks. These tasks are different pieces of work that various team members sign up to perform.

Another scenario: You are a software developer or a coach managing a software development team where there is a high proportion of discovery, creativity, or testing involved. Too much monitoring wastes time and suffocates programmers. Tracking does not increase the certainty of indicators because of the chaotic nature of the system. Too much data is meaningless. Not enough monitoring leads to blocks and possible idle time between assignments. Avoid all this by providing for precise quotes, plans, and proper monitoring; meet with the staff members for a short time (15 minutes) in a Daily Scrum Meeting. It will provide you with more accurate quotes, short-term strategies, appropriate tracking, a correcting mechanism to react to changes and adapt every 24 hours. Scrum Meetings typically occur at precisely the same time and place every day, so that they also serve to build a strong culture. The format of the Backlog and the blocks can vary, ranging from a list of things on a sheet of paper to software online representations. The trick to Scrum is pinning down the date at which we want completion for release or production, prioritizing performance, identifying available resources, and making significant decisions about architecture.

CHAPTER 5

Time to Grow

5.1   Time to Grow

Your system and behaviors need to be established in such a way that you can see all the action options you need to see when you need to see them. This is just common sense, but few people have their processes and their organization honed to the point where they are as functional as they could be. A few seconds a day is usually all you need for review, as long as you're looking at a sufficient amount of the right things at the right time. When you have access to a phone and any discretionary time, you ought to at least glance at the list of all the phone calls you need to make, and then either direct yourself to the best one to handle or permit yourself to feel OK about not bothering with any of them. When you're about to go in for a discussion with your boss or your partner, take a moment to review the outstanding agendas you have with him or her, so you'll know that you're using your time most effectively. When you need to pick up something at the dry cleaner, first quickly review all the other errands that you might be able to run en route.

Your most frequent review will probably be of your daily calendar, and your daily tickler folder if you're maintaining one, to see the *hard landscape* and assess what has to get done.

After you review all your day- and time-specific commitments and handle whatever you need to about them, your next most frequent area for review will be the lists of all the actions you could possibly undertake in your current context. If you're in your office, for instance, you'll look at your lists of calls, computer actions, and in-office things to do. This doesn't necessarily mean you will be doing anything on those lists; you'll just evaluate them against the flow of other work coming at you to ensure that you make the best choices about what to deal with. You need to feel confident that you're not missing anything critical.

The real trick to ensuring the trustworthiness of the whole organization system lies in regularly refreshing your thinking and your system from a more elevated perspective. That's impossible to do, however, if your lists fall too far behind your reality.

The Weekly Review is so critical that it behooves you to establish good habits, environments, and tools to support them.

You may be the kind of person, however, who doesn't have typical weekends. Whatever your lifestyle, you need a weekly regrouping ritual. The people who find it hardest to make time for this review are those who continuously have on-demand work and home environments, with zero built-in time or space for regrouping.

You need to assess your life and work at the appropriate horizons, making the appropriate decisions at the appropriate intervals in order to have a clear outcome, and avoid unnecessary expectations. That's a lifelong invitation and obligation to yourself, to fulfill whatever your unfinished destiny or intentionality happens to be.

Over the years, I have discovered, through my own experience as well as through being intimately involved with scores of people in their day-to-day worlds, that being grounded and in control of the mundane aspects of life produces a rich field of natural inspiration about our higher level stuff.

Ultimately and always, you must trust your intuition. There are many things you can do, however, that can enhance that trust.

At any point in time, the first thing to consider is, what could you possibly do, where you are, with the tools you have? Do you have a phone? Do you have access to the person you need to talk with face-to-face about three agenda items? Are you at the store where you need to buy something? If you can't do the action because you're not in the appropriate location or don't have the appropriate tools, don't worry about it.

Try this simple exercise: Divide your computer-required actions into those that don't require an Internet connection, those that do, and those that are just surfing. *Actionable time is very different from clock time.* The factor in choosing an action is how much time you have before you have to do something else. If your meeting is starting in 10 minutes, you'll most likely select a different action to do right now than you would if the next couple of hours were clear. Additionally, there are many times when you have been head down in some mentally intensive endeavor for a couple of hours, and you'd like to shift your focus and get some easy wins.

Although you can increase your energy level at times by changing your context and diverting your focus, you can do only so much. The tail end of a day taken up by a marathon budget-planning session is probably not the best time to call a prospective client, start drafting a performance review policy, or broach a new and sensitive topic with your life partner. Just as having all your next action options available allows you to take advantage of various time slots, knowing about everything you're going to need to process and do at some point will allow you to match productive activity with your vitality level. I recommend that you always keep an inventory of things that need to be done that require minimal mental or creative horsepower. When you're in one of those low-energy states, do those things.

You may be doing things on your action lists, doing things as they come up, or processing incoming inputs to determine what work needs to be done with them, then or later, from your lists. But many people let themselves get sucked into the second aforementioned activity—dealing with unplanned and unexpected things that show up—much too quickly and let the other two slide, to their detriment. In fact, much of our life and work does just show up at the moment, and it often becomes the priority when it does. It's indeed true for most professionals that the nature of their job requires them to be instantly available to handle new work as it appears in many forms. If you let yourself get caught up in the urgency of the moment, without feeling comfortable about what you're not dealing with, the result is frustration and anxiety. Many people use the inevitability of an almost infinite stream of immediately apparent things to do as a way to avoid the responsibilities of defining their work and managing their total inventory.

People often complain about the interruptions that prevent them from doing their work. But interruptions are unavoidable in life. When you become elegant at dispatching what's coming in and are organized enough to take advantage of *weird time* windows that show up, you can switch between one task and the other rapidly. You can be processing e-mails while you're on hold on a conference call. Research has now proven that you can't multitask, that is, put consciously focused attention on more than one thing at a time. If you are trying to, it denigrates your performance considerably. If your head is your only system for place holding, you will experience attempted multitasking internally, which is psychologically impossible and the source of much stress for many people. If you have established practices, however, for parking still incomplete items midstream, your focus can shift cleanly from one to the next and back again, with the precision of a martial artist who appears to fight four people at once, but who in reality is only rapidly shifting attention.

Your ability to deal with surprise is your competitive edge and a key to sanity and sustainability in your lifestyle. But at a certain point, if you're not catching up and getting things under control, staying busy with only the work at hand will undermine your effectiveness. And, ultimately, in order to know whether you should stop what you're doing and do something else, you'll need to have a good sense of all your roles and how they fit together in a broader context. The only way you can have that is to evaluate your life and work appropriately at multiple horizons.

There is magic in being in the present in your life.

Getting things done, and feeling good about it, means being willing to recognize, acknowledge, and appropriately engage with all the things within the ecosystem of your consciousness.

In order to create productive alignment in your life, you could quite reasonably start with a clarification from the top down. Decide why you're on the planet. Figure out what kind of life and work and lifestyle would best allow you to fulfill that contract.

Because everything will ultimately be driven by the priorities of the level above it, any formulation of your priorities would most efficiently begin at the top. I have learned over the years that the most important thing to deal with is whatever is most on your mind. The fact that you think it shouldn't be on your mind is irrelevant.

5.2   Role of the System Administration

The job of a system administrator is to keep one or more systems in a useful and convenient state for users. On a system, the administrator and user may both be the same person. Or the system administrator may be halfway around the world, supporting a network of systems, with a user being only one of the hundreds of users. A system administrator can be a person who works part time, taking care of a system, or a user within the system. Or the administrator can be several people, all working full time to keep the system running.

Complex systems are often so spread, at different scales, that quite different descriptions are required to capture the full essence. A theory of system behavior at, say, the microscopic level of system calls need not resemble a theory for the behavior at a macroscopic scale of larger entities, such as patterns of user behavior. Both are needed to understand the whole hierarchy of things going on.

In taking a high-level view, one conceptually separates an average view from a detailed low-level view; this is like the procedure of information hiding in creating directory structures or the use of subroutines in programming.

In computer science, a basic model proposed for a computer is that of a dynamic *community* of processes and resources, coupled with an external environment of users.

A set of networked hosts, sending external messages, is no different, for present purposes, from a single virtual host with internal inter-process communication.

Time plays a crucial role in the knowledge of system administration since computing systems are dynamic systems. Several important time scales emerge and are essential in separating the details of the response of the system to different influences. The passage of system time in a computer system occurs through the iteration of the fetch–execute cycle; thus, the time development of a computer is discrete at the microscopic level. Over more extended periods, this discreteness is unimportant, however, and the system may readily be approximated as a function of continuous time.

Finally, we must consider the importance of using "time blocks" in our daily, weekly, and monthly scheduling. As we have seen in this chapter, we can only grow professionally by incorporating time management tools within clearly defined time slots. Distractions, low attention span levels, and, in general, any external input that can break cycles of forty-five minutes / one-hour workflows should be avoided at all costs.

CHAPTER 6

Time Management

6.1 A Refresh on Time Management Essentials

The first step to time management in out-of-balance times is to recognize the possibility beforehand. Stress is reduced should you plan for out-of-balance times.

Maintaining control of your time at work requires you to develop some ways to manage appointments, meetings, and other work interactions, so they are as efficient and productive as possible.

Money is not the scarcest and most valuable resource—time is. There are loads of approaches to make more money, but there is no way to add more minutes to an hour. You have a limited amount of this precious commodity, so you need to protect it and invest it as though it is your trust fund.

The solution is to ask for more money for your time. Some workers have a whole lot of control over their hourly income and may, therefore, charge more per hour for their services. However, the simple reality is that most people do not have the luxury of raising their income at will. To increase your hourly price, you need to choose whether you will work toward earning more money or earning more time. Then focus on performing high-value actions to accomplish that goal; the process of finding the necessary actions or items you can invest your time in can help you alter your hourly rate. The decision of how to increase your hourly worth—whether to work toward earning more cash in the same time or generating the same amount of money in less time—depends on your circumstances.

All the time in life is a trade. You are trading your time for something you would like, want, or need. I hope that I have the option to trade away things I do not need to perform for things I do want to do. The test is based on your value of time and enjoyment of a particular action or activity. If you have a variety of free time during the weekend and you enjoy being out in the yard, paying someone else to cut your grass may be a money–time trade that has no value for you. With leisure activities, your choice hinges on whether you would like to do them whatsoever. Just as understanding and comprehending that your life goals help you attain powerful time management skills, the effective use of your time goes a long, long way to shorten the journey to those aims. By investing your time with consideration and care, your journey toward your dreams is sure to be smoother. An old time management adage states that for every minute you invest in planning, you save 10 minutes in execution. Spend 1 hour planning your trip, and you will free up 10 hours—to achieve better business results, reduce stress, and add quality time at home. The best way to achieve your goals is to prioritize them and develop an ordered plan to reach them. A universally recognized method for optimizing productivity, called the *80/20 rule*, has proved auspicious time and again, for more than a 100 years.

Most productive people have yet another common trait: They treat everything in life as an appointment. These individuals value their time and the actions to which they commit, whether business or personal. They give importance to their duties, commitments, and activities by writing them down and giving them a time slot, whether they are one-time occurrences or regular actions. They make appointments with themselves.

Generally speaking, just 20 percent of those things you spend your time doing produce 80 percent of the outcomes that you wish to attain.

Before you can do any strategizing, you need to have a good, honest look at how you use your time. For folks who struggle with time management, the issue, by and large, lies in the crucial steps of analyzing and planning. Observe the following:

- Current use of your time
- Personal productivity trends
- Interruptions

After you identify the tasks and activities that you will need to accomplish to reach your objectives, assign a value to those goals so you can decide how to order your daily task list. You can make this decision because you have got a distinct idea about how you rank your priorities.

For a system administrator, your goal is to improve the provider's performance, whether you are supporting frontline sales staff or helping the corporate leadership in directing the company toward profitability.

Extra measures to consider include the following: Write down every-thing you will need to accomplish today. Do not try ranking the items at this point. You merely want to mind dump all the to-do activities you can think of.

Medium-level tasks are those activities that may have a somewhat negative consequence if not completed today. Low-level tasks do not have any penalty if not completed today, followed by the tasks you can del-egate. These are actions that somebody else can take on.

If you have trouble ordering several top priorities, begin with just two: Weigh them against each other—if you could complete only one task now, which of the two is most crucial? After you identify and order your priorities, you put them into time slots on your weekly calendar, bro-ken into 15-minute segments. This procedure is commonly called *time blocking*.

To begin, you need a daily calendar or Google Doc Calendar split into 15-minute increments. On that new program, start by dividing your day; draw a clear line between personal time and work time. The more you do it on paper, the more tangible the time-block program becomes. Start with the activities that are a regular part of your job and then factor in the priorities that are not routine.

One way to determine your effectiveness in time blocking would be to check results. Note-taking can be done both electronically, like on Evernote, or by the more conventional pen-to-paper format.

The primary reason for the absence of this kind of practical value-added thinking is the dearth of efficiently structured and usable systems for managing the potentially infinite amount of detail, which could show up because of the technically unlimited amount of notes and reminders allowed by note taking apps, and online calendar systems,. That's the reason my approach will be bottom up. If you do not feel in control of your current, actionable obligations, you'll resist concentrated planning; an unconscious pushback occurs. As you start to employ these approaches, however, you might find that they free up space for enormous creative and constructive thinking. If you have systems and customs ready to leverage your thoughts, your productivity can expand exponentially.

What follows is a set of practical methods to facilitate the natural, informal planning processes I recommend. Although these suggestions are all based on common sense, they're not followed by the majority of people nearly as often as they should be. Put them to use whenever and as frequently as you can, rather than saving your thinking for large, formal meetings.

The majority of the results you have identified for your projects list will not need any front-end planning, aside from the sort you do in your head, fast and obviously, to think of the next action on them.

For these, you'll need a more specific application of one or more of the other four phases of the natural planning model: purpose and principles, vision/outcome, brainstorming, and coordinating. The second type—the projects for which ideas show up, ad hoc, when you're on a beach or in a vehicle or a meeting—want to get a proper place in which these related ideas can be captured. Then they can reside there for later use as required.

There are most likely a few projects you can think of today, off the top of your head, that you know you need to have more objectified, fleshed out, and under control.

Some of the projects that have your focus at the moment will require you to prepare a free-form believing; the mindset that allows athletes to be "in the zone" and keep constant quick decision making during high-stress situations where emotional decisions draw the line between a won and lost game.

It would be best if you decided where and how you need to do this action, to know which action list to put it on.

You may have some jobs for which you have already collected notes and miscellaneous support team, and you will need to sort through them and get them into a more structured form.

Often the next progress to be made on project thinking is to establish a meeting with the folks you'd love to have involved in the brainstorming and decision making.

Don't lose any thoughts about projects that could prove helpful. Often you'll think about something you don't wish to overlook when you're in an area that has nothing to do with the job.

I have never seen any two projects that needed the same amount of structure and details to get them under control. So it wouldn't be effortless to make any one program that would suffice for most. There are multiple sorts of digital tools that will be extremely helpful. Most professionals are familiar with word processing applications, spreadsheets, and presentation programs, any of which may be the optimal way to structure project plans or components, especially after the goal, vision, and brainstorming phases are handled. The kinds of applications that are far more useful for free preparation and brainstorming are mind-mapping and outlining applications. I use an electronic mind-mapping tool for most of my projects in order to do focused brainstorming and to capture random thoughts about the plans, since they show up ad hoc.

Typically, the last mind map itself is a sufficient organization for me to feel comfortable that I have the project under control. Most good word processing programs also provide this functionality. The beautiful thing about these programs is that they can handle a wide range of sophistication—from the most straightforward bullet points about organizing a celebration to creating the structure for a whole book you are writing.

For those who have become increasingly digitally oriented, it's tempting to try to eliminate paper. Theoretically, that shouldn't be an issue, with all the digital note-taking, scanning, and character-recognition tools out there. However, handwritten note-taking isn't going away, for multiple reasons, not the least of which is the universality of the tools and the assortment of graphic representations available. We tend to believe differently when we express with different gear, and several people find that writing and drawing by hand unwrap a broader palette of ideas. Additionally, paper-based materials allow us to be reminded of relationships, information, and perspectives more readily than that which we can see at any one time on a computer screen. I know of many digitally savvy people who've returned to using paper planners because they found them more comfortable to use to organize their thinking and reminders.

6.2   A Deep Dive into Time Perception

Time psychophysics has examined questions, especially about concise duration experiences, for many decades.

Simultaneity is experienced if two auditory stimuli occur less than about 2 to 3 ms (longer for visual stimuli). Successiveness is experienced only at slightly longer durations. However, temporal order judgments cannot be made until the interstimulus interval is about 20 to 30 ms. These judgments rely mainly on automatic processing of stimulus information in sensory systems of the brain, as well as on neuronal networks that subserve these kinds of experiences and judgments. There is an extensive literature on these issues, but it is not a significant focus in this book. Earlier, as well as more recent, evidence clearly supports some general conclusions. The auditory system is more sensitive to short interstimulus-interval information than is the visual system. This fine-tuning (i.e., the concise interaural time difference) of the auditory system is essential in localizing sound sources. The visual system relies on well-known parietal lobe systems in localizing stimulus locations, and these do not have to be very fine-tuned in the temporal domain. Here is where sensory (across-senses) differences are typically substantial and significant. However, with durations longer than about 3.0 to 5.0 ms, perceptual and memorial differences are typically small and not significant (see later).

The transition from past to present and future involves a changing present. In this view, time flows like a river. It is a fundamental perception of the flow of time.

The perceptual flow of events, occurring at 3.0 to 5.0 s, involves all perceptual modalities. One can easily show this in the auditory modality by playing the first four notes of Beethoven's famous Fifth Symphony at an interstimulus interval of 3.0 to 5.0 s; most people do not recognize it, and those four notes do not sound much like music.

The experience of happening (change) for both walking (spatial change) and toasting (color change) depended on the ISI (initial stimuli response). Research data suggests that happening is a time (frequency)-dependent phenomenon. The flow of time (events) begins to be lost at about 3.0 s, and this percept is almost wholly lost at an ISI of 7.0 s.

The flow of events is a time percept, a property of the frequency at which its percept occurs. People experience a flow of time or flow of events, and it is a perceptual illusion. It is an illusion partly because, in modern physics, time does not *flow*. Our brains are, of course, part of the physical universe.

Consider durations longer than about 3.0 to 5.0 s. Present-time, or experienced duration, judgments are theoretically and empirically different from past-time, or remembered duration, judgments. Present time (prospective judgments of time in passing) involves a situation in which a person knows that duration is relevant and essential.

People remember less recent events as relatively more recent. They also base past-time estimates on two main kinds of processes—distance based and location based.

In distance-based processes, a memory trace is retrieved and experienced in terms of apparent recency. In location-based processes, an event is retrieved along with contextual associations (e.g., other events that occurred at about the same time). Forgetting of many time-based (episodic and autobiographical) details is the norm.

Time-based prospective memory involves remembering an intention to perform an action at a specific future time. Time-based prospective memory requires timing processes similar to those in prospective timing: attending to time (and concurrently also to events) and also remembering an intention and when to perform it. In other words, explanations of time-based prospective memory require an attentional-gate model or some similar model. Event-based prospective memory may involve some processes similar to those involved in time-based prospective memory, as well as others.

Psychological time relies on sensory, perceptual, attentional, and memory processes at different time scales. Psychological time is influenced by many different factors, such as attentional processes and contextual changes.

In modern physics, time is simply a slice of nonflowing space-time. For humans and other animals, times past, present, and future are remembered, experienced, and anticipated in ways other than those dictated by physicists.

From a structural perspective, it can be demonstrated that events in the world around us display a high degree of temporal organization at all levels of analysis. Many of the body's physiological processes are entrained in the circadian day–night cycle and the pattern of sleep–wakefulness, which, in turn, influence many behaviors and our overall level of functioning. In addition, many of the events we frequently encounter display a spatial array that is structured in and over time. Music, speech, body movements, and walking gaits are among the many events in which the sequence of notes, words, or actions unfolds with a characteristic rhythm and tempo over a given time span. This particular arrangement not only influences how an event is perceived and remembered but also the overall accuracy with which the event's velocity and total duration are subsequently judged. Beyond this more microlevel, temporal patterning can also be identified within more global and social frameworks of life. The types of activities we perform in everyday existence vary in cyclic patterns over a day, week, and year and thereby provide a scheduling scheme that serves to coordinate subpopulations of individuals. Different cultures have different conceptualizations of time, which can be reflected in the types of metaphors used to describe time as well as the overall pace of life.

Another dimension that exerts a significant influence upon everyday behavior is a temporal perspective and one's relative orientation toward the past, present, and future. Many clinical psychologists argue that this orientation is central to one's mental well-being and the degree of ego strength displayed in coping with life's difficulties. Indeed, it has been found that disturbances in temporal perspective are correlated with both delinquent and criminal behavior and certain forms of mental illness.

The ability to accurately estimate the passage of time plays a vital role in daily activities, from the sleep–wake cycle to speaking to the ability to play musical instruments. We process time across a wide range of intervals, from milliseconds to 24 hours.

CHAPTER 7

Office Time

7.1 The Power of No

In the past two decades, people have embraced communication technology. But in many ways, these miracles of convenience have robbed workers of their ability to control their own time. Multiplying points of access—voice mail, e-mail, instant messaging, audio and video conferencing, social media, texting, and of course, the cell phone—can shackle you like a house-arrest ankle bracelet, sentencing you to a life term of continuous availability. Business colleagues can track you down on vacation, and friends can interrupt a vital client presentation. I'm not sure I'd describe this as progress, but it's inarguably a fact of modern life.

Consider this: Every one of these interruptions—no matter how small or insignificant—robs you of at least five additional minutes of productive time.

The most significant interruptions in your workday frequently come from within ourselves. Your co-workers pose a significant threat to your effective time management. What's doubly scary is that you don't always recognize your colleagues as threats. Hey, these folks are on your team—they're the good guys; they're there for you! However, it's essential to recognize the signs of danger from time-wasting co-workers. If not, you're at risk of falling to friendly fire. The modern workplace is often designed as an open-office, open-door, and open-exchange environment. Workers are connected through instant messaging, and employees text with co-workers in the office as well as out in the field—the days of working remotely and virtually are here to stay. The physical proximity of working in an office can be a help or a hindrance. Few, if any, employees are granted an office with a door, and most workers are parked in open cubicles, often with partitions that do little to block views (and definitely not the noise) of co-workers. It's supposed to manifest a more unified effort and team spirit, I guess. But it doesn't do much to protect you from your teammates' intrusions on your time. Unfortunately, the same open-door philosophy that allows employees to drop in on their supervisors at will is often carried throughout the workplace.

It's essential to be available to staff to address issues and offer encouragement. However, a manager who loses control of the border may discover that the flow of employee communication is akin to a circus parade with a never-ending line of elephants connected by trunks and tails.

A popular preemptive tactic that managers have followed since the first workplace self-help books came out, management by walking around, puts the time control back in the manager's domain. It suggests that making the rounds on a scheduled basis allows you to establish your availability and deflect those interruptions that could otherwise come later. Instead of getting snagged on the way to get a cup of coffee, you proactively seek out your staff, asking how their projects are going or if they have any concerns or issues you can help with. A good manager can make the rounds as well with virtual staff members. By setting a time to call, text, or instant message remote team members daily or weekly, you can open up communication but also limit and control the time. Most virtual or remote staff members feel somewhat disconnected from other parts of your team; however, the regular check-ins, even by instant message, can create a lifeline of connection.

Establish your scheduled interaction time as an open-office time for staff to drop in. Or require employees to make appointments to meet with you during that time.

One danger in setting up a specific drop-in hour is that it puts you in a state of waiting. You may not get any takers of your time, but your ability to focus on any other work is more challenged because you're expecting to be interrupted at any moment. To avoid this, I've implemented scheduled-appointment hours in my office.

Used effectively, the use of the telephone, text, instant message, social media, and e-mail can enhance performance, increase productivity, boost profitability, and expedite career growth. But there's a flip side: Because modern communication allows for more natural interruptions, it creates a more significant loss of production, performance, profitability, and advancement than ever before. And to a certain extent, these accessible forms of electronic communication have taken many people hostage.

When you stop to open every e-mail as soon as it arrives or answer the phone every time it rings, or the ding of the text or instant message, you are, in essence, multitasking, trying to perform one or more tasks simultaneously. And, as I frequently point out, multitasking is a myth.

I am a firm believer in working offline. There's no way I can resist the temptation to check my e-mail every time my computer tells me a message has arrived. The interruptions of texts, instant messages, and social media would take over my day. During your offline time, turn off your e-mail notifications/disconnect from the Internet and mute your cell phone. Schedule your e-mail, text, and social media time, and devote a reasonable time block to take care of it.

If you compose your e-mail in a word processing program, you gain yet another advantage: This tactic serves as a safety precaution—you won't inadvertently shoot off a critical e-mail before you're delighted with it!

Let your voice mail or assistant take phone messages. Voice mail is your not-so-secret weapon for dodging phone interruptions and taking back your time. If your system has a do-not-disturb button, push it, or put your ringer on mute, and you won't be tempted to ponder who called. If you're an executive, forward the calls to your assistant for a time or ask the receptionist to let your callers know that you're in an appointment and will call them back. Additionally, give yourself time when you turn off your cell phone.

The administrative staff has total control of the drawbridge that grants access to the fortress. They should have an aggressive approach to allowing people access to you. You need to clearly identify to your staff who is to be granted access and who is not. Only a few people should pass easily through the gate; the rest should be screened thoroughly to see whether another team member can assist them first.

If you have to put off doing something because of time limitations, make it one of the routine day-to-day tasks. These are the low-value, low-reward actions that produce limited results, something you can most likely delegate to someone else. Be cautious about postponing the growth and big-picture aspects: Even though they tend to be longer term in scope, if you don't stay on top of these issues, the consequences can be significant.

The best bosses have already assessed themselves and their staff and are using the information to minimize team weaknesses by maximizing everyone's strengths.

If you have employees who report to you, being a good time manager isn't enough. For maximum benefit, your staff members also need to improve their time management skills. Coaching your employees is part of your job, and improved time management makes everyone's job, including yours, much more manageable.

Strong knowledge of proven time management principles can increase the volume of work your staff can complete in an 8-hour day. Additionally, employees need to have a solid knowledge of their job and the responsibilities expected of them.

Skilled time managers usually acquire their expertise through practice, trial and error, and daily use of techniques (as well as through a few failures). Your staff has to develop time management expertise in the same way. Employees who have time-related skills—such as the ability to organize themselves and their work area and use tools such as Evernote, Google Calendar, a CRM (customer relationship management) solution, time blocking, and organizers—are likely more efficient.

Maintaining a positive attitude is a choice, however, and it's one you have a right to expect your employees to make. A poor attitude leads to negative results, and—you guessed it—more wasted time. Even if skills and knowledge are on the weaker side, the right attitude makes for faster and more significant improvement in time management skills.

The most significant increase in productivity comes from selecting the right activities on which to spend your time.

As soon as you understand a staff member's problem areas, the next step is to develop a plan to overcome these challenges and turn the employee into a productive, efficient dynamo. One of the first items on your agenda, when you want to overhaul employees' time management skills, is to establish goals. If you can, schedule weekly or at least regular sessions with an employee, each session lasting at least a half-hour. In addition to checking the benchmark status and getting an update from the staffer, you can introduce a new time management technique. These sessions can help you keep tabs on the individual's progress and inspire the employee to stick with the effort. Establish routines and then help employees develop their routines. When you make a commitment to help an employee improve, you invest time of your own, and you understandably don't want to give up, even if things don't appear to be progressing.

Time management skills are critical to the success of an individual and the team. If you have an employee whose failure to meet time management goals is affecting the success of your area, and if you've done everything you can (as outlined in this chapter) to help the employee attain time management skills, you may find yourself obliged to let the individual go and replace him or her with someone who has his or her time under control—or who shows promise of developing the skills.

7.2   Beyond Time Management

Nowadays, the majority of people have abandoned traditional alarm clocks in favor of using tablets to wake up every morning, making your smartphone the very first (and last) thing that you see every single day. It's simple to wake up and check your e-mail to see what's going on. Unfortunately, this makes you start your day on the wrong foot. Instead of focusing your energy on your main projects and tasks, your mind becomes distracted by other individuals' wants and desires. Rather than starting the day proactively, you've now flipped the switch into a reactive style. To take advantage of your mental clarity, schedule a time to check your e-mail when you are not at your peak. Your projects and activities should take precedence when you are most concentrated. By making this one simple change and adequately utilizing your prime time, you can save countless hours weekly. If you're using your smartphone as an alarm clock, turn off all automated push alarms, so you are not tempted to sneak a peek when you receive an alert. The moment you escape bed, grab your phone and put it in your laptop bag or someplace where you won't be inclined to check it: They stay out of sight, out of mind. Do the same with your computer and tablet. Switch off all e-mail alarms and do not open any other programs that aren't relevant to the jobs you are working on. If you're still struggling to achieve daily goals, try using an alarm clock instead of your smartphone and turn your smartphone off before going to bed. Leave your telephone off while you are working; turn it on again once you come to a natural stopping point in your project or task. If you still cannot break the habit, download the Freedom app, which blocks distracting websites and apps during specific periods so you can concentrate on the task at hand. To prevent unnecessary correspondence, even if you do keep your phone on during these no-e-mail intervals, activate your cell phone's Do-Not-Disturb mode (available on iPhones and many Androids), together with an autoresponder that informs others what times you reply to e-mail throughout the day.

Additionally, obtaining a well-crafted e-mail signature with essential details such as your name, address, telephone number, site, office hours, and social media profiles is a superb way to prevent unnecessary e-mails and queries. In case you have a job that needs you to be always connected, ask that crucial communications come through another medium, like a text message or telephone call. This will allow you to get your important messages without needing to dive into e-mails first thing each morning. If your company requires you to be accessible via e-mail, set up e-mail filters that will sort your messages based on priority, so only essential communications are observable on the main window. Now that you're on the path to creating healthful e-mail customs, it is time to get your inbox in order. Just like the physical files that you maintain for essential documents in your work and home, you ought to have a system for organizing necessary and critical e-mail correspondence. After you prioritize and create folders, you get a virtual filing system set up that makes it easier to track and reply to your messages. Setting up folders additionally prevents your inbox from becoming your digital to-do list, and it reduces stress by storing e-mails to a minimum.

7.2.1   Filtering

As soon as you create an organizational program to your e-mail inbox, consider it one step further by setting up automated filters and prewritten answers to help streamline your workload and also keep your order in place should you subscribe to newsletters. No matter what your occupation is, you most likely experience the very same queries, time and time again. The easiest way to manage this would be to craft a series of response templates such as

Thank you for asking about our return policy." By writing your answers upfront, you save yourself the bother of having to think something up each time and unveil the same solutions over and over again. When you have your canned responses, simply copy and paste them in a Word document so you can easily retrieve them.

7.2.2   Unsubscribe

How much time do you spend deleting unwanted promotional and industry-related e-mails? Whenever you are going through your e-mail daily, take a few added seconds and unsubscribe yourself out of any unsolicited correspondence. Most companies make this easy by adding an unsubscribe button at the bottom; it generally takes just a couple of clicks. Additionally, make sure you uncheck the subscribe box when making purchases on the Internet— you'll avoid future promotional e-mails from ending up in your inbox.

7.2.3   No Joint Accounts

Sharing an e-mail account generates an overcrowded area where you always have to browse and sort through each other's messages. If they are not sorted through, this could lead to e-mails that sit in the inbox because each party will assume it is for the other. Having a joint account makes it hard to keep things organized since you don't understand whether the other person would like to maintain correspondence, delete it, or file it off.

7.2.4   Personal Recommendation

Now I program 30 to 60 minutes at the end of every month to clean up and clean out any previous e-mails, files, and folders. I download any necessary attachments and documents and transfer them to a folder on my computer. While I recommend creating as many folders as you want to systematize your e-mail accounts, scanning roughly 100 folders (a lot of which I haven't utilized in years) takes time.

7.2.5   Daily Goals

Meaningful work is often disrupted by menial tasks that accumulate and obstruct our paths to actual goal fulfillment. Before starting with daily goals, it is crucial to identify the ones you would like to place for the long term because without recognizing what you are attempting to accomplish, you will not know where to start or what to do each day. To get your big picture into consideration, think of what you would love to accomplish and then break it down to smaller action steps so that you may create a road map to get there.

7.2.6   Time Blocking

One of the reasons time blocking is so powerful is that all your everyday activities and also the time required to complete each are best accounted for, leaving no room for grief. To begin with time blocking, first, write a prioritized to-do listing. Many unique programs may be used for the actual time blocking, such as Google Calendar, a traditional newspaper planner, or perhaps a spreadsheet populated with dates and times. Just make sure you are looking at only 1 day at a time, not the whole month. Then start filling in each 30-minute block with this day's errands, appointments, and must-do tasks, beginning with your most important priorities. While doing so, make sure you overestimate how much time you think it will take to finish an assignment. To get the most out of the method, it is ideal for planning a minimum of 1 day. It is irrelevant which scheduling medium you choose—what's important is that you are using a system that makes you more efficient.

7.2.7   Offline or Online?

To discover a balance between being connected and using your time, you need to establish boundaries so that there's a clearly defined separation between the two. When you are creating boundaries, consider your goals; this could help you determine the times and terms for when you use your device and when you do not. The easiest way to stop these annoying interruptions from stealing your valuable time would be to turn off your smartphone while you're working. However, if turning off your phone isn't an option, take some time to experience all your apps and turn off all of your push notifications. Maybe you tend to get distracted when you are overwhelmed, or any time you have a challenging project looming ahead. To prevent procrastination from seeping in, it's imperative to get organized, set deadlines, and eliminate surplus online action (unless your work needs to be always online, like in customer service, advertising, or technical support).

7.2.8   Long-Term Goals

Maintaining a long-term list can help you monitor your goals with time. While in many ways it seems somewhat like a typical to-do list, this one is much more fluid. Even on this list, however, prioritization is crucial. Ensure you order your lasting things according to importance, include deadlines where applicable, and check the menu weekly to ensure nothing is forgotten. When a job is urgent, remember to break down the steps to reach it and add them to your calendar. For those of you who use an efficient strategy to life, try altering your perspective. Instead of taking on another job and pushing yourself to fatigue because of an idealistic image in your mind, reflect on how you feel. Picture yourself in the future, looking back at your life. Are you creating the types of memories that you imagine in your dreams?

7.2.9   Meetings

Every player involved in a meeting serves a significant role. Whether you're planning the meeting or you are an attendee, it's crucial that you understand what your intended duties are so that you can be a more effective and productive contributor. If you are the assembly creator, plan on developing your schedule early and dispersing it ahead of time. Items to pay attention to include the objective, date, time, location, attendees, whatever attendees should prepare beforehand, action items, and the order of things to be discussed. Whichever role you play at the meeting, ensure you know the purpose and that there is a well-structured agenda to back it up. As a participant, it's imperative that you see the meeting's aim, who is involved, and your primary role in the discussion. All meetings should have a designated beginning and ending point. For bigger audiences and intricate issues, restrict the number of things to be discussed since these factors generally require additional time to get through. If you're the meeting secretary, communicate in your invite that you will start promptly at the specified start time. Don't wait for late individuals. As the organizer, you will be accountable for ensuring that the meeting agenda and goals are followed. Stay on topic, always. Do not be a distraction to other people. Bring positive energy into the meeting. No cross-talk is allowed; set the principles before the meeting (define if it's an announcement, an all-hands session, or an open Q&A session).

Double-check camera and sound configurations at least 10 minutes before the session starts. Test out your location ahead of the time. Make eye contact, look at the camera when speaking. Share the scope of the meeting via meeting invite or e-mail to make the most out of the assembly and make sure that you cover all necessary points. Invite meetings e-mails to follow the *exact same structure* of project e-mails. They need to include the following three points:

- Action
- Subject and goal(s)
- Deadline to achieve the target(s)

These three points will also define the subject line.in the e-mail You're going to convey what action is needed, what your message is about, and when the task has to be finished.

CHAPTER 8

Tools

8.1 Time Management Tools

Success is a short race. Bring the right habits and repeat them daily; a light discipline over time will help you stay focused (on the habits).

Don't gamble with your time, and you are placing a bet you can't afford.

We need to expand our thoughts to find the type of answers we need in order to master time management. Any process full of questions, project sprints, tedious review sessions, and continuous updates is a process that will never go beyond the doable and will always be hard to scale and fully succeed outside its framework.

Time will always mirror facts: Who we are and where we want to go is determined by what we do and what we achieve. It is very time expensive to reverse or mask the reality of facts.

A *goal-setting scheme* for small projects:

- Next-month achievement: one specific achievement I want to get done next month
- One-year achievement: the achievement I want to get done next year based on the next-month achievement
- Six-month achievement: the achievement I want to get done in the next 6 months based on the 1-year achievement
- Weekly achievement: the achievement I want to get done every week is s based on the 6-month achievement.

Time-managing systems: In reply to "What time-managing tool do you use?" answers are usually calendars, mobile apps, monthly planners. "How do we choose our time management system?" Most of the time, the answer is the format, usability, availability rather than the function.

Since we experience time (mostly) in one direction, why not use the most productive time of the day to do one thing? We can't buy time, rewind time, or extend time, but we can save it, invest it, and experience it. We consider time as a precious asset that continuously runs out; yet, we seem unable to use it wisely. Is it because our thoughts and planning are more concerned about future outcomes and past mistakes? Or, is it because we engage in forecasting-oriented decision making only when resources and *natural results* seem to have vanished?

Behind successful businesses and great achievements is always a very defined organization of time: the time to do or be and a time to manage and direct the results obtained from doing or being.

Try to be creative in the morning and analytical in the afternoon; practice time framing. Time framing is about defining blocks in time and making sure those blocks are protected from distractions, unnecessary priorities, and past–future thoughts. For example, you should always have at least 30 minutes during the week to review your monthly goals. Most of us already practice time blocking every year—when we think, visualize, and plan a vacation and make sure to have those days off in our work calendars. Now, imagine investing the same time and effort people put in *vacation planning* to plan priorities management, goals planning, resources reviewing, and risk forecasting. It is hard to do if we have no personal involvement such as material rewards or emotional reward, but we are talking about life planning, and, as we previously said, we are continually running out of time, so why not put ourselves in the right mindset? We cannot get more time, but we can leverage what we have left.

Take some time to observe yourself in your personal and work life. Does life happen or do you make it happen? When you face a challenge, what is your approach? Do you own it or get on with it? Do you find a solution or wait and hope? No matter what, time will keep being experienced in one direction, and you will be accountable. Either you are full of personal excuses and fight reality or face it and acknowledge the reality. The productivity outcome of your time investment will always be proportional to how much you get involved with events, decisions, projects regardless of how prepared or qualified you are. That is why an individual willing to learn and new skills, and grow both personally and professionally is always the choice of successful companies. Being involved with time rather than trying control is a sign of openness and willingness to grow.

About the Author

Giulio D'Agostino is an Award winner entrepreneur, system administrator, and cybersecurity consultant with more than twenty years of experience in Cloud Computing, Software as a Service, and Publishing fields. Previously worked for Google, Apple, Hewlett Packard, and Salesforce.com, Giulio has lectured at the Technical University of Denmark - DTU, Griffith College Dublin, Web Summit 2016/2017, worked as Irish Tech News contributor, and he is currently working as System Administrator for SaaS and cloud-based remote connectivity services company LogMeIn Inc.

Index

OTHER TITLES IN THE ENTREPRENEURSHIP AND SMALL BUSINESS MANAGEMENT COLLECTION

Scott Shane, Case Western University, *Editor*

- *A Cynic's Business Wisdom: Winning through Flexible Ethics* by Jay J. Silverberg
- *Dynastic Planning: A 7-Step Approach to Family Business Succession Planning and Related Conflict Management* by Walid S. Chiniara
- *From Starting Small to Winning Big: The Definitive Digital Marketing Guide For Startup Entrepreneurs* by Shishir Mishra
- *How to Succeed as a Solo Consultant: Breaking Out on Your Own* by Stephen D. Field
- *Small Business Management: A Road Map for Survival During Crisis* by Andreas Karaoulanis
- *Native American Entrepreneurs* by Ron P. Sheffield and J. Mark Munoz
- *The Entrepreneurial Adventure: Embracing Risk, Change, and Uncertainty* by David James and Oliver James
- *On All Cylinders, Second Edition: Succeeding as an Entrepreneur and a Leader* by Ron Robinson
- *Cultivating an Entrepreneurial Mindset* by Tamiko L. Cuellar
- *From Vision to Decision: A Self-Coaching Guide to Starting a New Business* by Dana K. Dwyer
- *Get on Board: Earning Your Ticket to a Corporate Board Seat* by Olga V. Mack
- *Department of Startup: Why Every Fortune 500 Should Have One* by Ivan Yong Wei Kit and Sam Lee
- *Family Business Governance: Increasing Business Effectiveness and Professionalism* by Keanon J. Alderson

Concise and Applied Business Books

The Collection listed above is one of 30 business subject collections that Business Expert Press has grown to make BEP a premiere publisher of print and digital books. Our concise and applied books are for...

- Professionals and Practitioners
- Faculty who adopt our books for courses
- Librarians who know that BEP's Digital Libraries are a unique way to offer students ebooks to download, not restricted with any digital rights management
- Executive Training Course Leaders
- Business Seminar Organizers

Business Expert Press books are for anyone who needs to dig deeper on business ideas, goals, and solutions to everyday problems. Whether one print book, one ebook, or buying a digital library of 110 ebooks, we remain the affordable and smart way to be business smart. For more information, please visit **www.businessexpertpress.com**, or contact **sales@ businessexpertpress.com**.

www.ingramcontent.com/pod-product-compliance
Lightning Source LLC
Chambersburg PA
CBHW061835220326
41599CB00027B/5289